Life without Strife

Joyce Meyer

Charisma® HOUSE

LIFE WITHOUT STRIFE by Joyce Meyer
Published by Charisma House
A part of Strang Communications Company
600 Rinehart Road
Lake Mary, FL 32746
www.charismahouse.com

Library of Congress Catalog Card Number: 00-109029
International Standard Book Number: 0-88419-734-4

01 02 03 04 05 06 9 8 7 6 5 4 3 2
Printed in the United States of America

Contents

Spirit of Strife

For where envy and strife exist,
confusion and every evil will be there.
—James 3:16

Helmet of Pride	Hammer of Judgment
Breastplate of Unrighteousness	Cloak of Deception
Sword of Bitterness	Boots of Anger
Shield of Hate	Speaking Forth Lies

Interactive Study Guide Questions

Jesus Christ desires for you to live in the love and excitement of anointed relationships, free from division, disappointment, confusion and hurt. But too often strife enters into our lives, our homes and our relationships, wreaking havoc and leaving us wounded and alienated from one another.

This special study edition of *Life Without Strife* by Joyce Meyer holds powerful revelation for overcoming the strife that stops Christians from realizing the promise of genuine, loving relationships. By following the interactive lessons, you will learn to recognize when strife is entering into your relationships. You will receive dynamic keys for discerning the roots and symptoms of strife. And best of all, you will discover how to defeat strife forever!

This interactive study guide edition will help you to find the freedom of peace and unity in your relationships so you can truly enjoy *Life Without Strife!*

My people are destroyed for lack of knowledge.
–Hosea 4:6

Who is blind but My servant?
–Isaiah 42:19

Introduction

I was once a servant of God who was being destroyed because of a lack of knowledge about strife. Strife is a spirit that is sent from hell to destroy. That spirit was a part of my life for too long.

I was always striving with something or someone. I did not understand the trap into which Satan had lured me. I loved God, was born again, was baptized in the Holy Spirit and had a call on my life to full-time ministry. But I lived in strife.

The Bible says a lot about strife and contention, which are actually the same thing. I believe that your eyes will also be opened as you read this book. More clearly than ever before, you will see the devastating, destructive effects of strife. My prayer is that you will see its effects so clearly that strife will never again be unrecognized and unconfronted in your life.

Today the spirit of strife is destroying churches almost faster than God can build them. Thousands of marriages are ending in divorce because of a spirit of strife. People are sick from the stress of dealing with strife. People sacrifice their prosperity for it and lose their jobs as a result of it. Businesses find themselves facing bankruptcy because of it. Strife throws thousands of children into a state of rebellion and confusion.

All of these things occur, yet people don't see the cause of their problems. How does Satan get in—especially in the lives of Christians who are supposed to have some protection from the negative things in life?

He gains an entrance through strife!

Strife does not have to destroy us.

Jesus gave us His peace for our protection. The Word says we are to "hold our peace" and "let peace be the umpire" in every situation (Exod. 14:14; Col. 3:15). We should "crave peace and pursue it," and be "makers and maintainers of peace" (Ps. 34:14; Matt. 5:9).

There are wonderful promises in God's Word for the peaceful. One of them is found in Psalm 37:37. "Mark the blameless man and behold the upright, for there is a happy end for the man of peace." Think of it. The man of peace will be happy!

Righteousness, peace and joy are the inheritance of the believer. The kingdom of God consists of these three things, but few who claim Christ as their Savior actually experience these benefits in their daily lives. Satan steals peace from them. He deceives, lies and beguiles believers through a lack of knowledge or the unwillingness to apply the knowledge we have.

If you are living in strife, this book will expose it. You will learn to overcome the spirit of strife and live the peaceful life God wants you to have.

One

Exposing Strife

The spirit of strife has an assignment from hell to bring destruction everywhere it goes. We cannot see this spirit, but we can certainly learn to recognize the symptoms of its presence. I believe strife is a bickering, arguing, heated disagreement or an angry undercurrent. The dictionary defines *strife* as "fighting; heated, often violent conflict; bitter dissension; a struggle between rivals; or contention."[1] Other descriptive words that identify strife are "quarrel, rivalry, wrangling, debate, provocation, factions."

Many people live in destruction due to a spirit of strife, but they do not recognize it as the root of their problems. Some believe the devil is behind the destruction, but they are unaware that they provide access for Satan through the door they're holding open for him.

A gentleman who attended my conferences regularly for many years related an incident to me that will help you see the danger of strife. One evening, this man and his wife had a heated argument. As bedtime approached, the Holy Spirit prompted the man to make peace with his wife. He was reminded of the Scripture verse that says we are not to let the sun set on our anger. (See Ephesians 4:26.)

He knew the right thing to do, but his fleshly stubbornness and pride were pressing hard in an attempt to prevent him from doing so. He tossed and turned, unable to sleep. Around 2 A.M. that morning the Lord spoke to him and said, "I am going to show you what you have allowed to enter into your house."

In a vision, the man saw a large, fierce demon spirit wearing heavy armor. The man could see each piece of the armor and understand its symbolic meaning. The spirit wore the helmet of pride and the breastplate of unrighteousness. He carried a sword of bitterness and a shield of hatred. From his belt hung a hammer of judgment. He wore a cloak of deception, and his feet were shod with boots of anger. He entered, speaking forth lies. (See illustration on page *iv*.)

Strife opens the door for all kinds of problems.

> For wherever there is jealousy (envy) and contention (rivalry and selfish ambition), there will also be confusion (unrest, disharmony, rebellion) and all sorts of evil and vile practices.
>
> —JAMES 3:16

This is a powerful truth! It reveals that if we can keep strife or contention out of our lives, we will also keep out other problems such as confusion or rebellion. The Holy Spirit revealed to me that much of the rebellion seen in our young people today is a direct result of widespread strife in their homes between their parents.

We are told that over one-half of all marriages end in

divorce. I can safely say that an abundance of strife precedes the severance of a marriage relationship. By the time we see a young person manifesting rebellion, often he has endured and lived in the midst of hundreds of arguments, watching and listening to his parents fight and bicker regularly.

A home atmosphere filled with an angry undercurrent instead of peace is an open door for rebellion in children. They rebel simply because the conditions in which they are living are incorrect. Deep inside they know something (strife) isn't normal, so they rebel against it. But the manifested rebellion expresses itself against everything. The violence in which they have lived makes them angry. They find all of life confusing.

Nothing seems to make any sense to them, so a deep-rooted bitterness is manifested in their behavior. They do not respect their parents' correction because the children view their parents as people who are out of control. Therefore, they believe their parents are unqualified to give instruction.

Years ago, before I dealt with the roots of strife within my own life, I often corrected my children for the same behavior I manifested. But I wouldn't let anyone confront me about it. Because I was easily angered, I was angry most of the time. And yet, when one of my children showed anger, I corrected my child's behavior. How could I expect my children to respect and trust me, to receive correction from me, when I was the one teaching them bad behavior through my own example?

Instructing a child verbally without backing up the teaching with corresponding behavior does more damage than good. A child becomes confused and rebellious when parents require him to do something that they will not do themselves. If a mother forces her daughter to do all the housecleaning while she does none, and continually makes messes for others to clean up, her daughter may do the work because she is forced, but she will rebel against such training in her heart. The same principle holds true with strife. A continual atmosphere of strife within the home creates a dysfunctional environment—one not filled with love and peace.

This does not mean that parents who argue occasionally in front of their children will cause a child to become rebellious. Almost any family has occasional disagreements. How parents handle the disagreements is the issue. It is healthy for children to see that people can have conflicts, admit when they are wrong and ask for forgiveness quickly.

Strife was a regular visitor in our home for many years. I had been sexually, physically, verbally and emotionally abused by my father from early childhood until I left home when I was eighteen. I had lived in the midst of a lot of violence and anger.

Because of the abuse I received at home, my entire childhood was filled with fear, embarrassment and shame. My father controlled me with anger and intimidation. He never physically forced me to submit to him, but he did force me to pretend I liked what he was doing. This, I believe, along with my inability to express my true feelings, left me deeply wounded.

I moved out while my father was at work. I married the first young man who showed an interest in me shortly after that. My new husband was a manipulator, a thief and a con man who was usually unemployed. He once abandoned me in California with nothing but one dime and a carton of soda bottles.

The result of this abuse caused me to be angry and quick-tempered. I had many internal problems that manifested in relationship problems. To put it plainly, I was very difficult to get along with.

As I grew in my relationship with the Lord, I began to desire peace. When I came to the point that I intensely hungered and thirsted after peace, the Holy Spirit began to teach me about strife and its dangers. I learned to recognize it and to resist the devil at its onset. I now treat strife like the plague—as a dangerous foe who will bring destruction if left unconfronted.

After one of my meetings, I was approached by a woman who told me how her entire family was being set free through my teaching tapes on strife. She said that after hearing me teach on strife, God revealed to her how the spirit of strife had been working deception in her family bloodline for generations. Her family had a history of conflict and divorces, with brother mad at brother, sister mad at sister and children hating parents.

She had purchased the entire teaching album on strife and began a study of the subject. She quickly learned to recognize strife and resist it. Her life became peaceful, and one by one her relatives were set free by the same truth.

> If ye continue in my word, then are ye my disciples indeed; and ye shall know the truth, and the truth shall make you free.
>
> —John 8:31–32, KJV

I believe many who read this book will see the truth that uncovers the hidden enemy of strife. Often people fight over minor issues—things that do not even make much difference. When strife gets in, everything seems out of control. People get enraged but often cannot even remember later how the problem started.

In our home and in our ministry, my husband, Dave, and I have learned to recognize the symptoms. Dave and I work in our ministry together and must make many decisions. Because our personalities are different, we often do not think alike on issues or see things in the same way.

We discuss many things, but we can recognize when our

discussions are being affected by strife. We work hard to keep strife out of our relationship and out of the ministry.

We deal with strife and people who are sowers of strife. Strife must enter through a person. When people come to work for us at Life In The Word, we tell them during their training that we will not put up with strife. We encourage them to beware of judgment and criticism that will open the door to strife. We advise them to take their opinions to the Lord—not to other employees. We train them to walk in love with other employees, being abundant in mercy and quick to overlook an offense.

You must never forget that strife is a spirit sent out from hell to bring destruction to every area of your life. If you desire to walk in victory, learn to recognize the spirit of strife and confront it. You can begin by confronting it in prayer, but you will also have to learn to confront strife as taught in Ephesians 6:12.

> We are not wrestling with flesh and blood [contending only with physical opponents], but against the despotisms, against the powers, against [the master spirits who are] the world rulers of this present darkness, against the spirit forces of wickedness in the heavenly (supernatural) sphere.

Learn to fight against the spirit of strife, and refuse to be fuel for it. Learn to identify the doors through which the spirit of strife will try to enter your life.

LIFE WITHOUT STRIFE

Study Questions

Chapter 1
Exposing Strife

Winning the victory over strife involves a spiritual battle with the enemy of our souls. Ephesians 6:12 says:

> We are not wrestling with flesh and blood [contending only with physical opponents], but against the despotisms, against the powers, against [the master spirits who are] the world rulers of this present darkness, against the spirit forces of wickedness in the heavenly (supernatural) sphere.

1. If Jesus Christ is called the Prince of Peace, who is the prince or principality of strife? ____________________

2. We've all been in circumstances that are full of strife. Describe some symptoms of a strife-filled . . .

   - ❑ Home ____________________
   - ❑ Church ____________________
   - ❑ Marriage ____________________
   - ❑ Other ____________________

3. What is the purpose for which Satan sends strife into your home? Your workplace? Your relationships? Your church?

4. The spirit of strife is the root behind many relationship problems experienced by believers. The vision of the spirit of strife revealed the following features:

- ❑ A helmet of pride
- ❑ A breastplate of unrighteousness
- ❑ A sword of bitterness
- ❑ A shield of hatred
- ❑ A hammer of judgment
- ❑ A cloak of deception
- ❑ Boots of anger
- ❑ Speaking forth lies

Think about a time when you became embroiled in a situation of strife. Without judging another person involved, ask God to show you how these characteristics became a part of your conversation and thinking patterns. What did you say or think during the controversy that was motivated by . . .

- ❑ *Pride* ____

  ____

  ____

- ❑ *Unrighteousness* (Did you seek to establish your own kingdom instead of God's kingdom?) ____________________

  ____

  ____

- ❑ *Bitterness* (Did you use phrases such as "you always" or "you never," which are signals of hidden bitterness?) ______

  ____

  ____

- ❑ *Hatred* ____

  ____

  ____

- ❑ *Judgment* (Did you assign motives and intentions to others when it is not possible to really know another's heart? Did you make judgments in other ways?)__________________

____

____

- ❑ *Deception* (Did you misunderstand the situation from another person's point of view, or did you form opinions without knowing all the facts? Did Satan plant thoughts in your mind about a person that were not completely accurate? Did you form opinions about another based upon gossip?) ____

____

____

- ❑ *Anger* (Did you speak words motivated by anger with the intention to hurt?)______________________________

____

____

- ❑ *Lies* (Did you lie, bend the truth, not present all the truth or in any way not be completely honest and open? Were you more interested in making your own point or getting your own way than in learning God's perspective in the matter?)____

____

____

Lord, help me to recognize strife and to learn to resist it. Help me to see the entrance of the spirit of strife long before it wreaks havoc in my home and life. Supply the grace to me so that I never fuel the spirit of strife in my life or in the lives of others. Amen.

Two

What Doors Open for Strife?

There are three doors that often swing open to allow the entrance of the spirit of strife into our lives. They are the doors of our lips, our pride and our debate. To resist strife, we must learn to lock these doors and refuse to open them at our enemy's approach through strife.

The Door of Our Lips

> And the tongue is a fire. [The tongue is a] world of wickedness set among our members, contaminating and depraving the whole body and setting on fire the wheel of birth (the cycle of man's nature), being itself ignited by hell (Gehenna).
>
> —James 3:6

Wrong words or words spoken at the wrong time can certainly start a fire. The more wrong words we pour on the fire, the bigger the fire. Over the years, I have learned to shut my mouth. The only way to stop a fire is to remove the fuel. Stop feeding it.

Many arguments could be avoided by someone simply deciding to say no more: "A soft answer turns away wrath, but grievous words stir up anger" (Prov. 15:1), and "A gentle tongue [with its healing power] is a tree of life" (Prov. 15:4). Words are containers for power! But they can carry either creative or destructive power. They carry the power of God or the power of Satan. A gentle tongue has healing power. A soft answer brings peace into the midst of turmoil.

When I sense strife at the door of my lips, I become much more careful with my words. If I continue speaking, I choose my words carefully. I am cautiously aware of the impact of voice tones and body language. Obeying the promptings of the Holy Spirit will always lead to victory. But stubbornly pressing on in our own way invites the devil to attack us.

> A [self-confident] fool's lips bring contention, and his mouth invites a beating.
>
> —Proverbs 18:6

I was always an expert at trying to convince others that my way was the right way. However, that led to and opened the door for strife. Many times I must back down, be quiet and trust God to take care of the situation. It is much more peaceful to let the Holy Spirit do the convincing.

Dave and I have learned to listen to the Holy Spirit in this area. There are times when we just do not agree. Dave is not hard to get along with. As a matter of fact, he is very adaptable and accommodating. But there are certain issues about which both of us feel very strongly, and nobody is going to convince either of us otherwise except God Himself. Sometimes God convinces Dave, and sometimes He convinces me. If I press the issue, trying to convince Dave, strife enters our lives. If I humble myself under the mighty hand of God and wait on Him, I have learned that He, and He alone, is able to convince my husband in certain situations. I would rather live in peace than get my own way all the time.

Speak out of wisdom rather than emotion.

> There are those who speak rashly, like the piercing of a sword, but the tongue of the wise brings healing.
>
> —PROVERBS 12:18

> A fool's wrath is quickly and openly known, but a prudent man ignores an insult.
>
> —PROVERBS 12:16

When someone insults us or hurts our feelings, we could quickly speak out of our wounded emotions. But it would be better to ignore the insult and let God deal with the person.

There are times to confront people, but it is vital to walk in peace and be sensitive to the Spirit of God in each situation. Sometimes I do not want to confront an issue, but God lets me know that I must. Other times I am all fired up and want to tell someone that they will not mistreat me or take advantage of me any longer. But no matter how much *I* want to confront that individual, the Holy Spirit persistently tells me to leave it alone.

Don't fuel the fire and open the door for strife. The tongue has the ability to start a bad fire in our lives. But even when wrong words ignite a flame, right words—or no more words—can put it out.

THE DOOR OF PRIDE

> By pride and insolence comes only contention, but with the well-advised is skillful and godly wisdom.
>
> —PROVERBS 13:10

Remember that contention is strife. This verse tells us that strife comes in through the door of pride. Even though wrong words may have opened the door to strife, it is a proud heart that refuses to be quiet in order to have peace. Pride demands that I have my say—I must have the last word.

Pride cannot lead me into victory. The Word of God teaches that pride will lead me into destruction. "Pride goes before destruction, and a haughty spirit before a fall" (Prov. 16:18). There is no hope of peace without a willingness to humble oneself. Thousands of divorces are obtained each year, and the only real problem in many of them is pride. Neither party was willing to say "I'm sorry." Neither was willing to say "I was wrong."

Obadiah 1:3 tells us, "The pride of your heart has deceived you." Pride will deceive a person and make him think he is right when he is actually wrong. I will discuss this deception in the next chapter.

Judgment, criticism, gossip and talebearing allow strife to enter, but all of these are birthed out of pride. Judgment says, "You are defective, but I am not."

An example of the destruction caused by pride and judgment can be found in Luke 18:10–14.

> Two men went up into the temple [enclosure] to pray, the one a Pharisee and the other a tax collector. The Pharisee took his stand ostentatiously and began to pray thus before and with himself: God, I thank You that I am not like the rest of men—extortioners (robbers), swindlers [unrighteous in heart and life], adulterers—or even like this tax collector here. I fast twice a week; I give tithes of all that I gain.
>
> But the tax collector, [merely] standing at a distance, would not even lift up his eyes to heaven, but kept striking his breast, saying, O God, be favorable (be gracious, be merciful) to me, the especially wicked sinner that I am!

> I tell you, this man went down to his home justified (forgiven and made upright and in right standing with God), rather than the other man; for everyone who exalts himself will be humbled, but he who humbles himself will be exalted.

Notice that pride will even follow us into the prayer closet. We may think we are praying about someone else's faults, but we may actually be operating out of a critical and judgmental spirit. We can be blinded to our weaknesses by a spirit of pride while attempting to correct another person.

The Door of Debate

History teaches us that the Pharisees spent a lot of time debating the Scripture. One of the words chosen to define strife is *debate.*[1] Christians often get caught up in strife through debating the Scripture. One person thinks one thing, and another believes something else. They each keep pushing their points and trying to convince the other. Soon the spirit of strife has entered, and relationships are damaged.

A while ago we hired three new employees, all very young and in need of some years to grow up in the Lord. Soon after they began, I received reports that other employees in the department sensed strife among the three new employees as a result of their debates on various portions of Scripture. Arguments that arise about Scripture are the result of spiritual pride. This is the most disgusting kind of pride to the Lord. His Word teaches against arguing, debating and contesting each other for first place.

Dave and I talked with the three employees and, happily, they were easily corrected. The door of debate was closed, and the strife ceased.

As long as we think we know *everything,* we do not know *anything.* When we believe we still have a lot to learn and stop passing out our opinions, we have finally come to the place where knowledge can begin. The apostle Paul stated:

> For I resolved to know nothing (to be acquainted with nothing, to make a display of the knowledge of nothing, and to be conscious of nothing) among you except Jesus Christ (the Messiah) and Him crucified.
>
> —1 Corinthians 2:2

Paul was not only a Pharisee, but he called himself the "son of Pharisees" (Acts 23:6). He was one of the chief Pharisees and extremely well educated. Yet, he says he would rather forget all he ever thought he knew in order to "know Christ and Him crucified." Over the years, I have found that I have to be nailed to the cross with Jesus regularly if I am going to stay out of pride. I have to "know Christ and Him crucified."

Too often, we don't understand statements like that in the Word of God, so we pass over them and miss a very important lesson. The Book of Romans says we will not reign with Him if we do not suffer with Him.

> And if we are [His] children, then we are [His] heirs also: heirs of God and fellow heirs with Christ [sharing His inheritance with Him]; only we must share His suffering if we are to share His glory.
>
> —Romans 8:17

I now enjoy the glory of a peaceful life, but I had to go through the suffering of learning to swallow my pride and keep my mouth shut when the Holy Spirit directed me to do so. I had to learn that when I thought I was right—I was probably wrong.

LIFE WITHOUT STRIFE

Study Questions

Chapter 2
What Doors Open for Strife?

Defeating strife involves slamming the door shut on it. Let's direct our attention to the doors of strife.

1. What three doors do we open that allow strife to enter?
   - ❑ ______________________________
   - ❑ ______________________________
   - ❑ ______________________________

2. The Bible says that the tongue is fire (James 3:6). Describe a situation in which what you said started a fire that opened the door to the spirit of strife. ______________

   ____
   ____
   ____
   ____

3. What are some strategies to quench the fires of strife that our tongues create? ______________

   ____
   ____
   ____
   ____

4. Judgment, criticism, gossip and talebearing allow strife to enter, but they are all birthed out of one particular door. What is it? ______________

   ____
   ____
   ____
   ____
   ____

5. Describe a time when you believed you were praying about another person's faults, but in reality you were operating out of pride.____________________

6. The Word of God says, "Pride goes before destruction, and a haughty spirit before a fall" (Prov. 16:18). Write about a time when your heart became lifted up in pride and later you experienced a fall. ____________________

7. What does Bible teach about being strongly opinionated according to 1 Corinthians 2:2?____________________

8. A certain amount of suffering is necessary to grace us to swallow our pride. Describe a situation in which you swallowed your pride and defeated the spirit of strife in your life.

Father, give me the grace and courage to examine my own motives and to easily admit when I have failed or I am wrong. I repent for all the times I have knowingly or unknowingly opened the door to strife through my words, my pride or my debate. I choose right now to slam those doors shut. And Lord, I ask You to give me supernatural sensitivity and grace to sense when those doors are about to open in my life. Give me the grace to close them immediately, before strife is released. And Lord, supply Your power to keep them shut so that I may walk in Your divine peace in all of my relationships. Amen.

Three

I Think I'm Right, but I May Be Wrong

The Book of James teaches us that if we have strife in our lives and pride in our hearts, the pride will rise up and tell us we are walking in truth when we are actually deceived.

> But if you have bitter jealousy (envy) and contention (rivalry, selfish ambition) in your hearts, do not pride yourselves on it and thus be in defiance of and false to the Truth.
>
> —James 3:14

On a practical level it means this: Dave and I can be in strife. Pride will convince me that I am right and the arguing and angry undercurrent are justified because Dave is refusing to listen to me.

Let me give you an example. One evening Dave and I were going to pick up another couple to take them out to dinner. We had only been to their home one time, and it had been quite a while since that first visit. On the way there, Dave turned to me and said, "I don't think I remember how to get there."

"Oh, well, I do!" I promptly told him, and proceeded to give him directions.

"I really don't think that is the right way to go," he said after listening to my directions.

"Dave, you never listen to me," I exclaimed. My voice tones and body language let him know that I did not appreciate being challenged by him. At my persistence, he agreed to go according to my directions. I told him they lived in a brown house on a cul-de-sac at the end of such-and-such street. As we drove, I gave him directions for all the turns.

As we turned onto the street where I believed their house to be, I noticed a bicycle lying on the sidewalk. "I know this is the right street," I said, "because I remember that bicycle lying there the last time we were here!" I was so convinced I was right that my mind was actually helping me in my deception!

Pride and deception always go together. We proceeded to the end of the street and—guess what! No brown house! No cul-de-sac! I was as wrong as wrong could be.

Have you ever been absolutely sure you were right about something? Your mind appeared to have a store of facts and details to prove you were right—but you ended up wrong. God uses experiences like that to show us how a prideful attitude opens the door and welcomes strife.

When Dave and I face such situations, God has enabled us to say, "I think I am right, but I may be wrong." It is absolutely amazing how many arguments we have avoided over the years by using that simple act of humility.

Believers are to avoid strife.

> And the servant of the Lord must not be quarrelsome (fighting and contending). Instead, he must be kindly to everyone and mild-tempered [preserving the bond

> of peace]; he must be a skilled and suitable teacher, patient and forbearing and willing to suffer wrong.
>
> —2 Timothy 2:24

A close look at the verse that precedes verse 24 gives us some insight into the "how to" of avoiding strive.

> But refuse (shut your mind against, have nothing to do with) trifling (ill-informed, unedifying, stupid) controversies over ignorant questionings, for you know that they foster strife and breed quarrels.
>
> —2 Timothy 2:23

I believe the verse is really saying this: "Stay out of conversations where no one knows what they are talking about, and everybody is arguing over nothing." So often people argue over things that make no difference to anybody. Notice the word *trifling* in verse 23. It indicates things that are unimportant and make no difference when considered with things that are really important.

In the past, Dave and I would argue over which actors and actresses were portraying the characters in movies or television programs we watched. It seemed to me that Dave thought half the characters in movies were played by Henry Fonda.

"Oh look," he'd exclaim as we watched a movie on television. "Henry Fonda is in this movie."

"That's not Henry Fonda," I'd answer back, and the arguing, bickering and strife would start. Intent on seeing who was right, we'd stay up much later than we should, just so we could see the credits roll at the end, and one of us could say, "I told you so!"

In the midst of one of these arguments, the Holy Spirit spoke to my heart. He showed me how trifling our actions were compared to the work of the kingdom that God had called Dave and me to. He showed me this was exactly what Timothy tells us to avoid.

I have used this Scripture a lot in various teachings, and people are always blessed by the Amplified Bible translation. In many situations nobody really knows what they are talking about—but everybody thinks they do. Pride wants desperately to look intelligent. The result is that the devil wins through strife.

Why do people strive so desperately to be right about things? Why is it so difficult to be wrong? Why is it so important to be right? Jesus was accused of wrongdoing regularly, yet never once did He attempt to defend Himself. He let people think He was wrong, and it did not disturb Him at all.

He could do so because He knew who He was. He did not have a problem with His self-image. He was not trying to prove anything. He trusted His heavenly Father to vindicate Him. For years I felt so bad about "who" I was. In order to feel confident at all, I had to think I was right all the time. I would argue to be right and go to great extremes to prove it.

Someone was always challenging me. I lived in frustration as I tried to convince everyone I knew what I was talking about. What a wonderful freedom it is not to have to do that any longer. Jesus came to set the captives free. People who argue over trifling issues just to prove they are right are definitely not free.

As my identity became rooted and grounded in Christ, I experienced more freedom in this area. My worth and value do not come from appearing right to others. They are found in the fact that Jesus loved me enough to die for me and bring me into a personal relationship with Him.

I gradually realized that great spiritual power is released through unity and harmony.

CHAPTER 3

I THINK I'M RIGHT, BUT I MAY BE WRONG

Strife gets us to fight to be right. The Bible teaches us that it is easy to deceive ourselves about the strife in our own hearts when we walk in pride. Strife will fill our minds with self-deception. We will be able to justify all kinds of wrong attitudes and behaviors, all the while being fully convinced that we are right.

The Bible says:

> But if you have bitter jealousy (envy) and contention (rivalry, selfish ambition) in your hearts, do not pride yourselves on it and thus be in defiance of and false to the Truth.
>
> —JAMES 3:14

1. Search your own heart and think very honestly about a time when you became embroiled in strife. Did you justify your actions? Describe that time. ____________________

   ____

   ____

   ____

   ____

   ____

2. Pride and deception go together. Asking the Holy Spirit to help you, recall a time in your life when your pride convinced you that you were right, but you were deceived nevertheless. Describe that time. ____________________

   ____

   ____

   ____

   ____

   ____

3. The Bible instructs believers to avoid strife. "And the servant of the Lord must not be quarrelsome (fighting and contending). Instead, he must be kindly to everyone and mild-tempered [preserving the bond of peace]; he must be

a skilled and suitable teacher, patient and forbearing and willing to suffer wrong" (2 Tim. 2:24). Recall a situation in which you were able to successfully avoid strife. Describe how you accomplished this. ______________________________

____

____

____

____

4. Jesus Christ was the target of endless attack from religious leaders. Yet He did not defend Himself. What was it about Jesus Christ that made Him able to let people think that He was wrong without defending Himself?____________________

____

____

____

____

Lord, I surrender to You my need to defend self, explain self, empower self and to always be right. I acknowledge that You alone are the only One who is right. And even if I feel right about some situations, it never justifies strife. I submit my life to You completely, and I choose to let You alone be my defender. Amen.

Four

Spiritual Power Is Released Through Unity and Harmony

There is no true spiritual power without unity and harmony. Great power is manifested in and through the lives of believers in the Book of Acts. The second chapter tells us why: "And day after day they regularly assembled in the temple with united purpose" (v. 46). They had the same vision, the same goal, and they were all pressing toward the same mark. "And when they heard it, lifted their voices together with one united mind to God" (Acts 4:24).

They prayed in agreement (Acts 4:24), lived in harmony (Acts 2:44), cared for one another (Acts 2:46), met each other's needs (Acts 4:34) and lived a life of faith (Acts 4:31). The early church as described in Acts lived in unity—and operated in great power. But the power of the church has lessened as the church split into various factions with different opinions. Denominations were never God's idea. Men who were unable to stay in agreement due to pride and other related problems caused the church to divide into many different groups.

I have decided that when we see Jesus face to face and ask Him who was right, we will find that none of us were 100 percent right. Only love holds people together in unity and harmony—love and a strong decision to do whatever is necessary to live in peace.

Paul urged people to live in harmony.

> Fill up and complete my joy by living in harmony and being of the same mind and one in purpose, having the same love, being in full accord and of one harmonious mind and intention.
>
> —Philippians 2:2

Just imagine the glorious, joy-filled lives we could have and the power available to those who pay the price to live as Jesus instructed.

What do I mean by "pay the price"? Look at the next verse.

> Do nothing from factional motives [through contentiousness, strife, selfishness, or for unworthy ends] or prompted by conceit and empty arrogance. Instead, in a true spirit of humility (lowliness of mind) let each regard the others as better than and superior to himself [thinking more highly of one another than you do of yourselves].
>
> —Philippians 2:3

This cannot happen without willingness to be obedient to the Holy Spirit in every situation where the opportunity for strife presents itself. The Holy Spirit leads us into peace—not turmoil. God's will for His people is that they walk in power, but there is no true spiritual power without peace.

Paul also urges the Ephesians to live in harmony.

> Living as becomes you with complete lowliness of mind (humility) and meekness (unselfishness, gentleness, mildness), with patience, bearing with one another and making allowances because you love one another. Be eager and strive earnestly to guard and keep the harmony and oneness of [and produced by] the Spirit in the binding power of peace.
>
> —Ephesians 4:2-3

Paul instructs the believers at Ephesus to live in harmony. In order to do so, they will have to make allowances for one another and overlook the mistakes and faults of others. The only way to do this is to walk in love. Love is self-seeking, but has the interest of others in mind.

Strife is the result of selfishness. It results from seeking to please ourselves—at any cost. The flesh, if not under the control of the Holy Spirit, does all in its power to have its own way: "Give me what I want, when I want it, the way I want it, and do it now!" That is the cry of man apart from the Spirit of God. To live in harmony, we must be willing to forgive quickly and frequently. We must not be easily offended. We must be generous in mercy, and we must be long-suffering (patient).

Hunger for Peace

I pray by the end of this book you will be so hungry for peace that you will do whatever you must to keep strife out of your life. The Word of God instructs, encourages and urges believers to keep strife out of their lives and live in peace. Why? Because God wants us to have blessed, powerful lives, and it is not possible without peace.

Paul tells us that the only striving we should do is to guard the harmony in our lives. (See 2 Corinthians 13:11.) If you want to strive at something, strive to keep strife out. In other words, be diligent. Do whatever you need to do to rid your life of strife. The quality of your life is greatly altered by strife.

Peace binds us to the precious Holy Spirit. God's Spirit is a spirit of peace. Jesus is the Prince of Peace. When He was ready to ascend to heaven, He told His disciples:

> Peace I leave with you; My [own] peace I now give and bequeath to you. Not as the world gives do I give to you. Do not let your hearts be troubled, neither let them be afraid. [Stop allowing yourselves to be agitated and disturbed; and do not permit yourselves to be fearful and intimidated and cowardly and unsettled].
>
> —John 14:27

After His resurrection Jesus appeared to His disciples. The twentieth chapter of John tells us about his appearances to His people. "Jesus came and stood among them and said, Peace to you!" (v. 19). "Then Jesus said to them again, Peace to you!" (v. 21). Even though His disciples were behind closed doors, Jesus stood among them and said, "Peace to you!" (v. 26). I think it is apparent that Jesus was saying, "Stay in peace!" Other verses tell us to "hold our peace" (1 Cor. 14:30, KJV).

Jesus gave us peace, but it will certainly slip away from us if we are not determined to hang onto it.

I recently received a letter from a couple who had attended a meeting we hosted in Florida. After twenty-seven years, the bondage of strife had been broken. Although they were Christians who loved each other, they had never been able to have peace in their relationship. They bickered, argued and could not seem to get along. They counseled others at their church, but they lived under condemnation because they could not do in their lives what they were teaching others.

The letter stated, "We reached a breakthrough because of your teaching on strife. We never really knew what the problem was. But now we do, and because of that revelation, we can live in victory."

> Better is a dry morsel, and quietness therewith, than an house full of sacrifices with strife.
>
> —PROVERBS 17:1, KJV

God is not pleased or satisfied with religious sacrifices in a house full of strife. For several years prior to discovering the truth about strife, our house was one of religious sacrifices with strife. We did a lot of religious or spiritual things, but lacked peace in our home.

I remember when we would fight and argue all the way to church on Sunday morning and then act spiritual as soon as we got around people we knew. I think we all have worn a "church face"—a face that is very different from the face we wear at home. We soon discover that God is not looking for phony Christians. He wants the real thing! Not just people who "talk the talk," but those who "walk the walk."

We talked about power, prosperity, healing and success back in those days, but we did not possess those things. It was like window shopping. We could see it, but did not know how to get it into our hands. Then God revealed to us that where there is strife, there will be no power or prosperity.

LIFE WITHOUT STRIFE

Study Questions

Chapter 4
Spiritual Power Is Released Through Unity and Harmony

Without unity and harmony, true spiritual power cannot be released.

1. The New Testament church of the Book of Acts is a picture of unity and harmony. Acts 2:46 says, "And day after day they regularly assembled in the temple with united purpose." Describe in greater detail the characteristics of the first Christian church using the following scriptures.

❑ Acts 2:44 ____________________________________
❑ Acts 2:46 ____________________________________
❑ Acts 4:31 ____________________________________
❑ Acts 4:34 ____________________________________

2. The key to such a powerful church is found in the following scripture:

> Do nothing from factional motives [through contentiousness, strife, selfishness, or for unworthy ends] or prompted by conceit and empty arrogance. Instead, in the true spirit of humility (lowliness of mind) let each regard the others as better than and superior to himself [thinking more highly of one another than you do of yourselves].
>
> —Philippians 2:3

2. Create a fictitious story about how wrong motives produce strife in a fellowship of believers. ____________________

____

____

____

____

____

____

____

3. Use Philippians 2:3 to write an ending to your story that restores a strife-filled situation back to one of peace and harmony. ________________________________

____

____

____

____

____

Dear Lord, by the power of Your wonderful Holy Spirit, reveal to me any attitudes that have created or fueled strife among my relationships at home, church, school or work. I humbly repent for not being a peacemaker. Show me how I can restore peace in relationships broken or damaged through offenses and misunderstandings. I make a new commitment to become a peacemaker whenever possible with Your help. Amen.

Five

How Does Strife Affect Prosperity?

We have many promises in God's Word that He will bless and prosper us. God is faithful and true to His Word, but His promises are often contingent upon our response:

> God is faithful (reliable, trustworthy, and therefore ever true to His promise, and He can be depended on); by Him you were called into companionship and participation with His Son, Jesus Christ our Lord. But I urge and entreat you, brethren, by the name of our Lord Jesus Christ, that all of you be in perfect harmony and full agreement in what you say, and that there be no dissensions or factions or divisions among you, but that you be perfectly united in your common understanding and in your opinions and judgments. For it has been made clear to me, my brethren, by those of Chloe's household, that there are contentions [strife] and wrangling and factions among you.
>
> —1 Corinthians 1:9–11

We like to read God's promises without the "buts" and "ifs." In this Scripture, Paul says God is faithful to His promises, but we must get along with one another. The Corinthians were people just like us, people in relationship with one another, arguing over trivial things they should have left alone.

> What I mean is this, that each one of you [either] says, I belong to Paul, or I belong to Apollos, or I belong to Cephas (Peter), or I belong to Christ.
>
> —1 CORINTHIANS 1:12

It sounds to me as though only the names have changed in today's arguments. Today we hear, "I'm Catholic, I'm Lutheran, I'm Baptist or I'm Pentecostal or charismatic." Read on to verse 13.

> Is Christ (the Messiah) divided into parts? Was Paul crucified on behalf of you? Or were you baptized into the name of Paul?

Paul was telling the Corinthians to keep their minds on Christ—not man. We must do the same. Sometimes we get so worried about what the other guy is doing that we forget all about Jesus.

The promises of God are true. He is faithful, but He does ask us to get along with one another. The blessings are abundant for those who will pay the price.

THE PRAYER OF AGREEMENT

> Again I tell you, if two of you on earth agree (harmonize together, make a symphony together) about whatever [anything and everything] they may ask, it will come to pass and be done for them by My Father in heaven.
>
> —MATTHEW 18:19

I can remember when Dave and I would pray the prayer of

agreement, but fail to see the powerful results we had been taught that we could have. As God uncovered the strife problem in our lives, I realized that He responded to the prayer of agreement when it was prayed by *people who agreed.* There wasn't any power in joining hands, bowing our heads and coming together in order to move God if we had been fighting all week.

The prayer of agreement will not work for someone who gossips about the pastor, then gets sick and asks the pastor to agree with him for a miracle in his body. The Amplified translation stated that this prayer is only effective when it is prayed by those who "harmonize together, make a symphony together " (v. 19).

God gave me a great example regarding harmony while I was ministering in a church. I asked the entire worship team to return to the platform, and then I requested them to sing and play a song of their choice. I knew, of course, that they would all choose a different song because I had given no instructions on what song to sing or play. As they sang and played, the sound was horrible! There was no harmony.

Then I asked them to play "Jesus Loves Me." It sounded sweet, soothing and wonderfully comforting. I made the point that disharmony is noise in God's ears, but living in harmony produces a sweet sound. The Lord appreciates our decision and sacrifice to live in agreement, and tells us to come together in agreement regarding a need and He will answer that prayer. There is power in agreement! There is weakness in strife!

Don't Block God's Blessing

> Behold, how good and how pleasant it is for brethren to dwell together in unity! It is like the precious ointment poured on the head, that ran down on the beard, even the beard of Aaron [the first high priest], that came

> down upon the collar and skirts of his garments [consecrating the whole body]. It is like the dew of [lofty] Mount Hermon and the dew that comes on the hills of Zion; for there the Lord has commanded the blessing, even life forevermore [upon the high and the lowly].
>
> —Psalm 133

I love this psalm. It verifies what I am trying to teach. It is good. It is pleasant. Life is enjoyable when people live in unity and keep strife out of their lives. There is nothing worse than a home or relationship filled with an angry undercurrent of strife. Unity is like the oil of anointing upon the high priest. Where there is strife, there will be no anointing.

Where there is unity, there God will command His blessings. Multitudes are seeking prosperity. They go to seminars on prosperity and read books on prosperity and success. This is good, for we need to be instructed and informed, but the Bible clarifies why prosperity eludes some people. It certainly eluded our family for a long while. We had all the right head knowledge—we gave and confessed and believed—but there was a missing link. We were living in strife and did not have any idea that it was blocking our blessing.

You may not be able to walk in peace with every single person you know. Don't be afraid that God will not be able to bless you. The Word says, "If possible, as far as it depends on you, live at peace with everyone" (Rom. 12:18). If you are a peacemaker, God's blessings will flow to you as they did to Abraham.

We know from Scripture that Abraham was a very rich man: "Now Abram was extremely rich in livestock and in silver and in gold" (Gen. 13:2). But let us look at one of the reasons riches and prosperity flowed into his life.

> Now the land was not able to nourish and support them so they could dwell together, for their possessions were too great for them to live together. And there was

> strife between the herdsmen of Abram's cattle and the herdsmen of Lot's cattle. And the Canaanite and the Perizzite were dwelling then in the land [making fodder more difficult to obtain]. So Abram said to Lot, Let there be no strife, I beg of you, between you and me, or between your herdsmen and my herdsmen, for we are relatives.
>
> —GENESIS 13:6-8

The first thing we see is that Abram (whom God later renamed Abraham) dealt aggressively with strife. Some people believe the strife among others in their group or under their authority is not their problem. I have learned if I have just two employees in strife, and I do nothing to eliminate it, that strife will spread throughout my organization. Good leaders must confront the issue of strife.

A mess behind the scenes will always cause visible problems. Some people may not connect the daily problems to the hidden strife because they are unaware of the dangers of strife. They may keep rebuking the devil and trying to resist their problems. In reality, the problem will never go away until the strife is removed and kept from returning.

Abram apparently knew this, so he dealt aggressively with the strife. The strife was happening between Abram's and Lot's employees (their herdsmen). Abram must have known that it would keep spreading until it affected his personal relationship with Lot, and he did not want that. If you are a leader, you have a responsibility to deal with people under your authority who are walking in strife.

I get weary from the need to deal with something all the time. I once said to Dave, "When will we get to the point when we are not dealing with someone or something all the time?"

"Never," he replied.

It's not really a problem for me to deal with issues now

because I do not let them upset me. I deal with them to the best of my ability, trusting God to help me treat people the way He would treat them.

When God began dealing with Dave and me to step out into full-time ministry, He spoke some things to us that we have lived by and from which we have seen good results. He said, "Keep the strife out of your life, out of your home and out of your ministry. Walk in integrity, and do what you do with excellence." That was many years ago. We have seen many ministries either fail or never grow beyond infancy due to failure in one or all of these three areas.

Strife is a killer! It kills the anointing, the blessings, the prosperity, the peace and the joy. Keep it out of your life! Be determined that strife is not going to steal from you what is rightfully yours as a child of God.

God spoke some powerful words to Abram, and Abram evidently was determined not to let strife come in and steal the blessings of God. I believe God will give you revelation as you read this book.

You may wonder why you are not prospering even though you are giving to God and believing His promises. Or, you may wonder why your ministry lacks power and is not growing. Do you have strife in your marriage, your home or your ministry? Are you a party to strife in your church or on the job? You must treat strife like some dreaded disease. Do all you can do to keep it from coming near you.

How did Abram handle the situation when strife arose between his herdsmen and those of Lot? Lot and Abram needed to separate so each could have enough land for their herds. Suppose two companies were sharing the same office space and both were growing. After a while, both companies would find that their employees were fighting over space, office machines, equipment and supplies.

They may have gotten along very well in shared facilities

while they were small, but now it's time for someone to move on. Otherwise, neither will grow any larger. It is like two plants in the same pot. If they become rootbound and have no more room to grow, both plants will fail to thrive in the small container.

Abram humbled himself and gave Lot the first choice of available land. It is interesting to me that he did this, because had Abram not included Lot in his blessings, Lot may have had nothing. Abram brought Lot with him and shared what he had with him. Let's look at Abram's response.

> Is not the whole land before you? Separate yourself, I beg of you, from me. If you take the left hand, then I will go to the right; or if you choose the right hand, then I will go to the left. And Lot looked and saw that everywhere the Jordan Valley was well watered. Before the Lord destroyed Sodom and Gomorrah, it was all like the garden of the Lord, like the land of Egypt, as you go to Zoar. Then Lot chose for himself all the Jordan Valley and [he] traveled east. So they separated.
>
> —Genesis 13:9–11

This was a potentially explosive situation. Here was an opportunity for the strife that was already affecting their herdsmen to affect Abram and Lot. Abram handled the situation with great wisdom, but it took humility and trusting God with his future to do so. First, he let Lot choose the land he wanted. How could Lot become angry when Abram was being so loving and considerate? Of course, Lot chose the best piece of land—the well-watered, fertile Jordan valley. He selfishly took the best for himself and did not consider Abram. Look at the results.

> Abram dwelt in the land of Canaan, and Lot dwelt in the cities of the [Jordan] Valley and moved his tent as far as

> Sodom and dwelt there. But the men of Sodom were wicked and exceedingly great sinners against the Lord.
>
> —GENESIS 13:12–13

Lot moved into a mess. Selfishness always leads to problems. Now let's examine how Abram fared from this deal.

> The Lord said to Abram after Lot had left him, Lift up now your eyes and look from the place where you are, northward and southward and eastward and westward; For all the land which you see I will give to you and to your posterity forever. And I will make your descendants like the dust of the earth, so that if a man could count the dust of the earth, then could your descendants also be counted. Arise, walk through the land, the length of it and the breadth of it, for I will give it to you.
>
> —GENESIS 13:14–17

Abram gave up, or "sowed," what he had in order to maintain godly principles. And the seed of obedience blossomed back to him in the harvest of God's promise to give him everything his eye could see. Abram trusted God to reward him for his obedience. So can we!

CHAPTER 5
HOW DOES STRIFE AFFECT PROSPERITY?

The Word of God says:

> Behold, how good and how pleasant it is for brethren to dwell together in unity! It is like the precious ointment poured on the head, that ran down the beard, even the beard of Aaron [the first high priest], that came down upon the collar and skirts of his garments [consecrating the whole body]. It is like the dew of [lofty] Mount Hermon and the dew that comes on the hills of Zion; for there the Lord has commanded the blessing, even life forevermore [upon the high and the lowly].
>
> —PSALM 133

1. Think back to a time when you were involved in a situation of strife. Describe how it felt. ____________________

   ____

   ____

2. Now think back to a time when you have personally experienced the kind of unity spoken about in Psalm 133. Write about how it made you feel. ____________________

   ____

   ____

3. Using the verse above, write about how strife hinders your prosperity. ____________________

   ____

   ____

4. Look up Romans 12:18. According to this verse, how do you walk in peace toward certain individuals who have no intention of living in peace with you? ____________________

   ____

   ____

   ____

5. According to Genesis 13:6-8, write how Abraham chose to be a peacemaker with his nephew Lot. ________________

____

____

6. Does this Bible story support the following statement: Just leave strife alone, and it will go away.

   ❑ Yes ❑ No

7. Why or why not? ________________________________

____

____

8. Why is it important to confront issues that create strife? _____

____

____

9. What principles can you glean from Abraham's actions with Lot to help you with your own relationship problems? _____

____

____

10. According to Genesis 13:14-17, Abraham had a God-given right to enjoy the rich lands that Lot chose. Describe the possible motives of both Abraham's and Lot's hearts and the long-term consequences of each of their choices. _________

____

____

Lord, show me how to diffuse potentially strife-filled situations. Teach me how to confront strife before it wreaks havoc. I give up my rights to You. Show me when being a peacemaker is more important than enjoying what is rightfully mine. Help me to choose the godly wisdom of harmony, unity and peace over the short-term benefits of getting my own way. Give me the wisdom to know when keeping the peace is of greater value in a relationship than being right or walking in what is rightfully mine. Amen.

Trusting God to Reward You

We can live our lives trying to take care of ourselves, or we can trust God to take care of us. When we enter into a relationship with God, we realize an awesome benefit—God wants to take care of us! We can retire from self-care.

I wore myself out mentally, emotionally and physically for years trying to take care of myself. Because of the physical and emotional abuse I endured as a child at the hands of people who should have taken care of me, and again during my first marriage, I thought that taking care of myself was safer than depending on anyone else to do it.

Before entering into a relationship with Jesus, many people are unable to trust others because of past hurts in their lives. God is not like other people. We can trust Him! Psalm 23:6 tells us, "Surely or only goodness, mercy, and unfailing love shall follow me all the days of my life."

Although God wants to take care of us, His hands are tied

by our unbelief and works of the flesh. He waits until we give up the job of self-care and place our trust and confidence in Him. Abram chose to operate in love in order to keep strife out. He also trusted God to take care of him instead of trying to take care of himself. Had he been trying to make sure he was treated fairly, he would not have allowed Lot to take first pick of the land.

The Danger of Self-Care

In my own life, I have discovered that it is very hard to walk in obedience to God and in love with my fellowman if my primary interest is that "I" don't get hurt or taken advantage of. How comforting it is to be assured of God's special care: "Casting the whole of your care [all your anxieties, all your worries, all your concerns, once and for all] on Him, for He cares for you affectionately and cares about you watchfully" (1 Pet. 5:7). This is a wonderful verse! Trying to take care of ourselves is one of the major root causes of strife.

Jesus trusted His Father to care for Him even when things looked bad for Him.

> When He was reviled and insulted, He did not revile or offer insult in return; [when] He was abused and suffered, He made no threats [of vengeance]; but He trusted [Himself and everything] to Him Who judges fairly.
>
> —1 Peter 2:23

When our circumstances seem out of control, or when others are hurting us or taking advantage of us, we naturally want to try to line things up in our favor. God wants to give us favor; therefore, we must trust Him for it. There are multitudes of promises in the Word of God, and they are all released through faith. Paul speaks of "the measure of faith" that is given to every man (Rom. 12:3, KJV). We have faith as a gift from God. It grows and develops as we use it. What we do with faith—where we plant it—is our choice.

If I choose to put my faith (trust and confidence) in myself, it is my right of free choice to do so. However, I will quickly learn that self-care does not produce supernatural results. We need supernatural results in our lives. The way to obtain them is by allowing God to be God.

God is a gentleman and will not just take over without being invited to do so. The law of faith mentioned in 1 Peter 5:7 is this: You stop trying to take care of yourself, and you release God to take care of you! God's provisions are available all the time, yet we may never enjoy them because of our unwillingness to retire from self-care.

Repeatedly, God's Word teaches us that God is our defense, our vindicator and our reward. (See Psalm 27:1; 59:9; Matthew 22:44.) He brings justice and recompense into our lives. (See Deuteronomy 32:35; Psalm 89:14.) Abram trusted God, and God rewarded him. God brought justice. He gave Abram so many descendants that they could not be counted. He gave him more land than he had before.

Lot, on the other hand, tried to take care of himself by choosing the best. He walked according to the natural. The people from the land that he chose were exceedingly wicked. He experienced devastation because of his selfish choice.

We experience the same devastation when we try to take care of ourselves instead of trusting God. Our enemies are powerful against us. We actually give them power over us through lack of faith in God. Having faith in myself will always bring failure. We are to "put no confidence . . . in the flesh" (Phil. 3:3). Not in our own flesh—or anyone else's.

God's Promises

> He shall call upon Me, and I will answer him; I will be with him in trouble, I will deliver him and honor him.
>
> —Psalm 91:15

There are three distinct promises for the believer who calls upon God.

1. God promises to be with us in trouble.
2. God promises to deliver us.
3. God promises to honor us.

Honor is a place of lifting up. When God honors a believer, He lifts him up or exalts him.

> Therefore humble yourselves [demote, lower yourselves in your own estimation] under the mighty hand of God, that in due time He may exalt you.
>
> —1 Peter 5:6

Refusing to try to take care of yourself produces humility, and that act of faith places the believer in the direct line of God's exaltation. When you trust God, you are in line for a promotion. God will honor you and reward you as you place your faith in Him.

Jesus trusted Himself and everything to the One who judges fairly.

> But without faith it is impossible to please and be satisfactory to Him. For whoever would come near to God must [necessarily] believe that God exists and that He is a rewarder of those who earnestly and diligently seek Him [out].
>
> —Hebrews 11:6

In the world's system, you work hard and then get your reward. In God's economy, you trust deeply and then receive your reward. I am not suggesting that we live in passivity, but I am strongly urging that we avoid all works of the flesh. Living by the arm of the flesh invites strife—within ourselves, with God and with our fellowman.

Consider the following scriptures. They will encourage

you to retire from self-care and look for God's reward as you place your faith in Him.

> After these things, the word of the Lord came to Abram in a vision, saying, Fear not, Abram, I am your Shield, your abundant compensation, and your reward shall be exceedingly great.
>
> —Genesis 15:1

> The Word of the Lord is perfect, His ordinances are true and right, by them we are warned (illuminated and instructed); and in keeping them there is great reward.
>
> —Psalm 19:8–11, author's paraphrase

> Men will say, Surely there is a reward for the [uncompromisingly] righteous; surely there is a God Who judges on the earth.
>
> —Psalm 58:11

> For I will surely deliver you; and you will not fall by the sword, but your life will be [as your only booty and] as a reward of battle to you, because you have put your trust in Me, says the Lord.
>
> —Jeremiah 39:18

> But when you pray, go into your [most] private room, and, closing the door, pray to your Father, Who is in secret; and your Father, Who sees in secret, will reward you in the open.
>
> —Matthew 6:6

Rather than trying to *make* someone treat me fairly, I have learned to pray for them and trust God to take care of me. Believers may pray in secret, often with tear-stained faces. But God will reward us in the open.

The Book of James clearly shows us how strife comes in through self-care.

> What leads to strife (discord and feuds) and how do conflicts (quarrels and fightings) originate among you? Do they not arise from your sensual desires that are ever warring in your bodily members?
>
> You are jealous and covet [what others have] and your desires go unfulfilled; [so] you become murderers. [To hate is to murder as far as your hearts are concerned.] You burn with envy and anger and are not able to obtain [the gratification, the contentment, and the happiness that you seek], so you fight and war. You do not have, because you do not ask.
>
> —James 4:1–2

I have discovered that people who are full of frustration are generally very difficult to get along with. For the years that I lived in works of the flesh, always trying to take care of myself, I also lived in strife. I was upset most of the time. I had a war going on within me, and I created quarrels and fights with those whom I had relationships with.

Self-care leads to strife. Trusting God leads to peace.

The strife resulting from self-care will ultimately destroy the people who have failed to trust in God for His care.

LIFE WITHOUT STRIFE

Study Questions

Chapter 6
Trusting God to Reward You

The Bible teaches that the Lord is our Shepherd. He has made a commitment to us to take care of us.

1. Write a few sentences about what this means to you. _______

2. Consider the concept of "self-care" for a moment. What does this mean to you? _______

3. In what ways are you unable to trust others because of past hurts? _______

4. Are there ways in which you have chosen to look to your own methods of self-care rather than trusting in Jesus, your Shepherd, to care for you? _______

5. Trying to take care of ourselves is one of the main causes of strife in our lives. Describe a situation in which your efforts at self-care have fueled strife in one or more of your relationships. _______

6. Rewrite 1 Peter 5:7 in your own words. _______

7. Read the following scriptures and write God's personal promise to you found in each one:

- ❑ Psalm 27:1 ______________________________
- ❑ Psalm 59:9 ______________________________
- ❑ Matthew 22:44 ___________________________
- ❑ Deuteronomy 32:35 ________________________
- ❑ Psalm 89:14 _____________________________

8. James 4:1–2 reveals how self-care leads to strife. It says:

> What leads to strife (discord and feuds) and how do conflicts (quarrels and fightings) originate among you? Do they not arise from your sensual desires that are ever warring in your bodily members? You are jealous and covet [what others have] and your desires go unfulfilled; [so] you become murderers. [To hate is to murder as far as your hearts are concerned.] You burn with envy and anger and are not able to obtain [the gratification, the contentment, and the happiness that you seek], so you fight and war. You do not have, because you do not ask.

Rather than trying to make someone treat you fairly, choose to pray for that person and leave his or her behavior with God. Write a personal commitment to God to leave the behavior of others in His hands. ____________________

____

____

____

____

____

Lord, release me from the strife-filled bondage of constantly struggling to make things happen for myself. Deliver me from the bondage of constantly feeling the need to protect myself. I choose to trust You to be a Good Shepherd who will care for me, watch over me and protect me from harm at the hands of others. In Jesus' name, amen.

Seven

Strife Destroys

I once heard the story of a Christian couple who lost everything they had in a fire. This loss caused confusion for those who knew them. Outwardly, they seemed to be doing everything right. Just graduated from a Bible college, they were preparing to go into full-time ministry. They had a bumper sticker, a tape recorder, everybody's tapes and a Jesus pin. They talked like people who knew the Word. The tragedy left questions in the minds of their friends and acquaintances. How could this happen to people who were walking in faith?

You may know of similar cases, but often what is happening behind closed doors goes unseen. Another student who attended Bible college with this couple revealed there was a lot of strife in their marriage. The couple often came to class with an obvious strain between them. It was not evident to everyone, but the third student had discerned that strife was present.

Later, they admitted that God had been dealing with them about their personal relationship and the strife in their home. They had not humbled themselves and come into obedience. A house full of sacrifices, yet with strife, is not pleasing to the Lord. (See Proverbs 17:1.) This young couple may have been sacrificing to go to Bible college, but none of the offerings of their flesh were satisfactory compensation for the door they opened to the devil through strife.

This couple knew the right thing to do. They knew what God was saying to them. He had been dealing with them, but they had not been heeding the warnings of God to them to "get the strife out of your home." Therefore, the devil took advantage of the open door and brought destruction.

Walk in Peace

In order to be successful in spiritual warfare, we must *wear* our shoes of peace—not just carry them around with us. God instructed us to put on the full armor of God. (See Ephesians 6:10–18.) God supplies us with all the armor we need to defeat the devil in every one of his strategies and deceits. But it's useless to us unless we put it on. We must keep it on, because "the devil roams around like a lion roaring [in fierce hunger], seeking someone to seize upon and devour" (1 Pet. 5:8).

Learning how and being willing to walk in our shoes of peace is one of the secrets of successful spiritual warfare. Taking authority over the devil with a loud voice does not replace simple obedience to the Lord. Jesus prayed:

> That they all may be one, [just] as You, Father, are in Me and I in You, that they also may be one in Us, so that the world may believe and be convinced that You have sent Me.
>
> —John 17:21

Going to Bible college is wonderful for those God leads to do so. Having a bumper sticker and a tape recorder can be beneficial. Wearing a Jesus pin on your clothes is a good way to spread awareness of our Savior. However, doing all of this and living in strife is a mistake.

Many frequently live in confusion, wondering why the promises of God don't work in their lives. The promises of God cannot just be "claimed." They must be inherited as we enter into a "sonship" relationship with our Father. The "sons of God" are those who are "led by the Spirit of God" (Rom. 8:14–15).

Judgmental Strife

I had a good friend whose husband was unsaved. She and her husband had a lot of strife in their home. My friend wore a frozen "charismatic" grin on her face all the time so, from outward appearances, everything looked good. However, she encountered one disaster after another.

Looking from the outside, it seemed so unfair. I was tempted to pray: "God, why aren't You protecting her? She is so sweet and does so much for others. She tithes and is in church every time the doors open."

Yet disaster seemed to plague her. Finally, everything really caved in on her—the roof of her house literally caved in! After this incident, she told me what was really wrong. She shared that God had been warning her to get the strife out of her home.

Her husband was not a warring man. He was rather passive—not very aggressive in anything. Yet his lack of interest in her, in their home, in their church and in their life was a constant source of irritation to her. She had strife in her soul concerning him. She judged him, and her attitude was one of continual nagging and critical comments. She kept strife stirred up. Any time we have strife within, it will come out in some way.

My friend told the Lord she just could not be quiet and let the man get by with his irritating behavior. She did not know it, but she was operating in self-care. God would have taken care of her, but she was too busy taking care of herself to realize it. She felt it was unreasonable for God to ask her to be a peacemaker in her home when she felt her husband was the problem.

She told me that she actually said to God: "I know what You are telling me, but I just cannot do it." Therefore, the door for the enemy to bring destruction through disobedience and strife was opened.

Strife Steals the Victory

I knew another couple who had continual problems with sickness, poverty, broken appliances and car repairs. They had no victory. Yet they tithed and attended church regularly. After years of this kind of destruction, they finally revealed in a counseling session that they had so much strife between them they had not slept together as man and wife for years.

It is easy for human nature to deceive itself by refusing to look at the "why" behind the "what." We must be willing to face the roots of strife within if we expect God to be able to defeat the destruction of the enemy externally.

Trials come for a variety of reasons. Disobedience is one of them. We can have problems in our life that have nothing to do with disobedience or strife. The devil may be simply attacking us, trying to destroy our faith. If we steadfastly resist him, we will come into a place of victory. But on the other hand, it is possible that strife is the root of our trouble. As we expose the deception of strife, face the truth and lay the groundwork in our lives for a miracle from God, He can bring a mighty deliverance.

His deliverance is available for the believer who is bound by strife, just as it is available for the church that is bound by strife.

LIFE WITHOUT STRIFE

Study Questions

Chapter 7
Strife Destroys

Strife can open the door of your life to the enemy's attacks and purposes against you.

> The Bible says, "That enemy of yours, the devil, roams around like a lion roaring [in fierce hunger], seeking someone to seize upon and devour."
>
> —1 Peter 5:8

1. Reflect on this verse for a minute. Can you describe a time in your life in which the enemy was able to rob you and destroy God's blessings because of a situation of strife? Write about it. ______________________________________

2. In Ephesians 6:10–18, God instructs us to wear the full armor of God to resist the enemy's attacks. According to Ephesians 6:15, this armor includes what kind of shoes? ________________

3. God requires obedience to His powerful Word. In light of our discussion about strife, rewrite the following verse in your own words. Jesus prayed:

> That they all may be one, [just] as You, Father, are in Me and I in You, that they also may be one in Us, so that the world may believe and be convinced that You have sent Me.
>
> —John 17:21

4. We may have problems that have nothing whatever to do with strife. On the other hand, we may be burdened with problems that have entered our lives through the door of strife. What situations, problems and circumstances in your life have been caused through the open door of strife? ______

____

____

____

____

Lord Jesus, please show me if I have opened the door in my life to the enemy through strife. I repent for any and all strife I have allowed into my life, and I ask You to help me to close the door to strife forever. Amen.

Eight

Strife Destroys Churches

Paul instructed the Corinthian church regarding God's faithfulness. He assured them God was faithful, and he taught the importance of living in harmony, unity and agreement. The Bible addresses the importance of strife-free living in many of its books. Consider this from Hebrews:

> Strive to live in peace with everybody and pursue that consecration and holiness without which no one will [ever] see the Lord. Exercise foresight and be on the watch to look [after one another], to see that no one falls back from and fails to secure God's grace (His unmerited favor and spiritual blessing), in order that no root of resentment (rancor, bitterness, or hatred) shoots forth and causes trouble and bitter torment, and the many become contaminated and defiled by it.
>
> —Hebrews 12:14–25

We are to want peace and to strive to live in it. Peace is to be a primary goal for the church. We are even to help watch over one another. If we see a brother or sister in the Lord becoming angry or getting upset, we should help restore them to peace if possible. This may be one of the meanings of the biblical instruction to be "peacemakers." These verses in Hebrews tell us that strife (or the absence of peace) leads to resentment, bitterness and even hatred. And if left unattended, it shoots forth and spreads.

Strife spreads like an infection or a highly contagious disease. That is why I have said that Dave and I treat strife like the plague. It causes trouble and brings torment to church members and to church leadership. It troubles and hinders the work of the Lord. Many become contaminated and defiled by it.

If a deadly plague should strike a household, the Department of Health would place the household in quarantine. Public notices would announce the house is contaminated. No one would be allowed in or near the house for fear they would be contaminated and defiled also.

Dave and I travel extensively in our ministry outreach programs. We have contact with a variety of churches and ministries. I can't number the ministries we have observed that are prevented from growing, and even destroyed, by the spirit of strife. Why is this so? Because God works in an atmosphere of peace. Satan and his demons work in strife and turmoil.

The Spirit of Offense

It is vital that the church receive revelation in this area. Satan works hard to get us upset. He sets us up to cause us to become angry with one another. He knows which buttons to push at just the right time. Remember, the devil is a strategist. He lays out a plan and does not mind working behind the scenes for long periods of time in order to accomplish his desired goal. He lies to people, setting them against each other.

He magnifies incidents and makes them appear to be much more important than they really are. A person can make a simple mistake and the devil will tell you they did it on purpose. He will make you believe people have plotted against you and are trying to hurt you on purpose. In reality, these people may not even realize how they offended you.

Perhaps an insecure woman thinks her pastor was not very friendly to her when she saw him at the shopping mall. It appeared to her that he was only "coldly polite," and tried to get away from her quickly. So her feelings are hurt, and she dwells on her hurt. The devil pounds her mind with remembrances of other times when the pastor was not very friendly with her—at least not as friendly as he is with other people.

She thinks, *He doesn't like me. As a matter of fact, he was downright rude. He is rather cold emotionally for someone who is supposed to shepherd God's people.*

The devil pounds at the woman's mind for days concerning this situation. She gets to the place where she cannot discern reality from fantasy. The situation is blown out of proportion completely in her mind, and she is in an internal rage.

Her family and friends can tell something is wrong with her, so they ask her about it. Although the Holy Spirit tries to tell her to keep her mouth shut, she relates the incident to them. Remember, they are only hearing her side of the story, which by now is very different from what actually happened.

Her opinions affect their opinions, and people begin to ask others if they think the pastor is unfriendly. Now, just as the Pharisees watched Jesus continually, hoping to catch Him in some wrong behavior, people watch the pastor and his attitudes toward them. If the man is not aggressively friendly with everyone, he will be judged, criticized and gossiped about.

The pastor senses that something is wrong. He feels "pressure" in the atmosphere at the church services, but he cannot put his finger on the cause. Given a few months, this kind of situation can turn into a "pastor's nightmare." A full-blown case of church strife that shuts down the anointing and blessings of God can develop from a simple misunderstanding.

Perhaps the pastor was not feeling good the day he saw the lady in the shopping mall. He may have been extra tired that day or preoccupied with financial pressure from the church building program. He could have been late for an appointment and only had time for a simple greeting. He has no idea that the insecure lady was offended and hurt, or that she is busy spreading strife throughout the church.

If you think this is a bit far-fetched, you are wrong. These incidents happen all the time in the kingdom. People become offended by minor things, and the devil uses these offenses to bring strife into the church. The work of God is shut down because the Holy Spirit will only work in an atmosphere of peace. The devil loves it. It's exactly the best atmosphere for his work.

Probably more damage is done by the spirit of offense than any other spirit. It is the believer's number one enemy. It opens the door for multitudes of deep, dangerous problems that few know how to deal with.

Such problems develop from carnal Christians—immature people who live by their feelings. They do and say exactly what they "feel." They don't operate in self-control and don't ask God to help them get over the hurt.

God Wants to Heal Our Insecurities

The Bible states plainly that we are to forgive those who hurt us—quickly, frequently and freely. Insecurity was the root of this woman's problem. A more secure or mature person would have taken a totally different view.

Insecure people carry a root of rejection. They need a lot of outward assurance that they are accepted. They lack feelings of worth and value from within, so they crave it from outside sources. They need people to affirm their acceptance by their actions and words. The enemy uses people with emotional wounds and scars to stir up trouble. Of course, they don't intend to cause trouble, they only want someone to make them feel good about themselves.

I have encountered many situations like this in my years of ministry. People who took offense because I did not pay enough attention to them. One woman was reportedly highly offended and felt I did not like her at all. When the story came to me, I was amazed! I liked the woman, and as far as I knew I was always friendly to her when I saw her. But she told people that I did not pay the same attention to her as I did to other people. She said I walked right past her without speaking. When I heard about a particular incident when she thought I had ignored her, the truth was that I had not seen her. I absolutely did not see her!

I asked the Lord why He didn't just make sure that I saw her and others like her. The Lord revealed to me that He "hid" the woman from me. He said, "She thinks that the thing she needs most in the world is for you to pay attention to her. But that is not what she needs. She needs to place her confidence in Me. When that is accomplished in her life, then I will allow her to have more attention from peers and people whom she admires."

This taught me a lesson. God wants to work in our lives. In order to do so, He must open up some old wounds so He can clean them out. As long as the woman's insecurities were being met by others, she would never get completely well. Each "fix" only prolonged her problem. It was like covering a major wound with only a small bandage. God wants to heal us, yet we keep putting bandages on the problem.

Insecurity is like a poison that affects every area of a person's life. Healing may be a bit painful, but it's better than being emotionally handicapped all your life. We must learn to trust God for the attention He knows we need.

If someone does not give us the attention we think we should have, what is a godly response? Respond with mercy and understanding. Give them the benefit of the doubt. Remember that love always believes the best. (See 1 Corinthians 13:7.)

Do unto others as you would have them do unto you. Would you want someone to judge you harshly, show you no mercy, gossip about you and spread strife in your church or organization? Of course you wouldn't! And neither would I. Peace can only be maintained—and strife kept out—by following the example of Jesus. How would He handle the situation you are facing?

Paul advised the Galatian church regarding the strife problem in the church.

> For the whole Law [concerning human relationships] is complied with in the one precept, You shall love your neighbor as [you do] yourself. But if you bite and devour one another [in partisan strife], be careful that you [and your whole fellowship] are not consumed by one another.
>
> —GALATIANS 5:14–15

His instructions are clear. Be careful concerning the problem of strife. If permitted to stay, it will spread. And if it spreads—you and the whole church may be ruined by it.

STRIFE HINDERS GOD'S CALLING

I know people who are not in ministry today because they took the devil's bait and let strife in. At one time they had the call of God on their lives. Not only did they let strife in—they invited it. I recall an incident that devastated many people in my ministry several years ago. I believe the individuals who started it hurt themselves even more than anyone else. Through this, and one other situation, I learned firsthand the dangers of strife.

In this first incident, I began to sense a "dead" feeling in my weekly meetings. There was a heaviness in the atmosphere. It's the feeling you get when demon activity is prevalent. Then I noticed that everything suddenly got silent when I approached groups of people who were talking. I had the strange feeling that I was intruding.

I tried to brush off the feeling because I believed these people were my best friends. People whom I had been close to for years suddenly seemed uncomfortable around me. Unseen walls were being erected everywhere. One day, some of the people I normally ate lunch with no longer wanted to go to lunch with me. When I talked with others about something I wanted to do in the ministry or about something I believed God was speaking to my heart, I would get silence and an uncomfortable feeling instead of the usual encouragement. It was as if everyone knew something I didn't know, and nobody wanted to tell me.

More than strife was involved. I learned later that deception, lies and other related problems were also active. When the lid blew off, as it always does, relationships were ruined and people backslid in their personal relationships with God. I believe, quite possibly, great ministries were side-tracked by the enemy through the effective use of strife.

What caused this devastation? A woman who had been practicing witchcraft for many years became involved in our church. She said she had finally realized that she was lost, and she was born again and filled with the Holy Spirit. She desired to get her life straightened out. Everyone was very happy for the woman. We all love to see people who were in deep bondage set free.

She got involved in several ministry areas quickly. She began attending the Bible college where I taught three times a week. She attended the weekly meetings at our home church. She joined an outreach ministry to the mentally handicapped and faithfully attended all the early morning prayer meetings at the church.

Everything looked right, but something felt wrong. When I say "felt" wrong, I am talking about spiritual feelings—not emotional ones. I had a check in my spirit about her. I could not get comfortable around her. I wanted to get away from her every time she came near.

One day, at a 6 A.M. prayer meeting, I walked by her and almost shuddered. I sensed within my spirit that she was praying for me—and I did not want her to. I later discovered she was praying, but she was speaking for the kingdom of darkness and releasing curses, strife and other forms of wickedness upon my ministry.

Because many totally uncharacteristic things started happening at the church, confusion engulfed the place. Accusations against people in leadership were flying everywhere. There were so many lies and gossip. It was hard to know whom to believe. People who had been attending the church for years left. Many of them held lay leadership positions.

Surprisingly enough, once the place fell into spiritual chaos, the supposed ex-witch disappeared. Satan had spread his lies. He had launched a battle against people's thoughts. He had tempted some with judgment and criticism, and they took the bait. They were gossiping behind the scenes. Strife was spreading. The angry undercurrent was flowing and many were swept away in the current.

It took months to repair the breach. Eventually, things got back to normal. Today the church is flourishing, and our ministry is being blessed mightily by God. Not only did we survive the attack, but we were made stronger through it. We learned a lesson that has kept us out of Satan's trap many times since.

However, some of the individuals involved have stagnated at that spot and gone no further. I learned the dangers of strife firsthand, and I have a holy violence in my spirit toward strife in any package.

Strife Hinders God's Anointing

The other case involved the first charismatic church that we attended. After just a few months in operation, this church was growing quickly, and the attendance had already reached four hundred or more people. The gifts of the Spirit were evident. The anointing of God and His fresh revelation were flowing to the people. Everything seemed to be the way it should be. But today the church is no longer in existence. What happened?

Strife got in! In this case it entered through the pastor and his wife. They were very sensitive and became offended when any of the people felt that God was calling them to leave the church and go elsewhere. If they happened to see the people who left, they were unfriendly to them.

They harbored unforgiveness in their hearts. They wanted to *control* the sheep—not lead them. If they wanted someone to get involved with a certain church program, but that person did not want to, he or she was met with a "cold shoulder" attitude.

I was corrected and ostracized for several things—once for teaching the Word. Dave and I had hosted a home meeting for two years prior to coming to this church. We continued the home group after we joined the church. The pastor thought Dave should be teaching the home meeting. Because we wanted to be obedient to the will of God, Dave tried to teach and I tried to be quiet. Neither one worked! I am called to teach, not Dave. No matter what man says or thinks, it only works right when we function as God intends.

One Christmas season, I wanted to buy ten thousand tracts and organize a group of ladies to hand them out at shopping malls once a week. I believed God had put it on my heart. All the ladies were friends of mine, and I was going to pay for the tracts personally. My goal was to distribute all of them in six weeks. I thought we could hand them to people inside the mall and put them on car windshields in the parking lot until the ten thousand tracts were gone. It never occurred to me to get permission from the pastor to do it!

The pastor chastised me, saying I would ruin my marriage if I did not submit to my husband. But Dave was not having a problem with me—the pastor was.

Another time, I was corrected for casting out devils. Finally, our name was removed from the weekly bulletin as an approved home for weekly home meetings. This kind of treatment happened to many other people in the church besides Dave and me. The pastor thought he was doing the right thing, but he opened the door for strife because of the way he handled the situation.

Dave and I wanted to leave the church and go elsewhere, but God kept telling us not to leave with anger or unforgiveness in our hearts. We were young Christians at the time, but we knew better than to harbor hard feelings in our hearts toward the pastor and other leaders in the church.

Week after week we waited for God to release us. Week after week we watched the attendance decline. One day I had a vision during my prayer time that I was attending a funeral. I did not understand the entire vision, but I realized the funeral was for the church. It was dying. When God finally released us, only about one hundred people were left. That number gradually dwindled to nothing, and they had to close the doors.

What happened? Strife got in and destroyed the church. This pastor's ministry was redeemed, and he later went on to be used by God in other ministries.

Satan Attacks the Babies

When I look back at that situation and at some of the people who were members of that church, I am amazed to realize how many of the people involved in that incident have well-known, national ministries today.

Satan had launched a major attack. Many of the ministries were not even birthed yet—except in the heart of God. Others were in the infancy stage. The devil wanted to destroy these ministries before they could destroy him. He wants to attack, and hopefully devour, the young. He attacks the babies and toddlers in the kingdom because they do not know how to defend themselves.

I am so thankful that God had someone praying for me. I may never know who it was, but I know someone's prayers were used to save us from the ravages of strife on more than one occasion. Never forget that strife destroys. It destroys marriages and relationships on every level. It destroys churches and para-church ministries. It destroys businesses. And it destroys people's health.

It is a peace stealer of the highest degree. If you can learn to recognize and deal with strife, you will stop a lot of intended destruction. We will look at one area of destruction due to strife—our physical health.

LIFE WITHOUT STRIFE

Study Questions

Chapter 8
Strife Destroys Churches

It is important to fellowship with other believers in Christ who are free from strife. The Bible says:

> Strive to live in peace with everybody and pursue that consecration and holiness without which no one will [ever] see the Lord. Exercise foresight and be on the watch to look [after one another], to see that no one falls back from and fails to secure God's grace (His unmerited favor and spiritual blessing), in order that no root of resentment (rancor, bitterness, or hatred) shoots forth and causes trouble and bitter torment, and the many become contaminated and defiled by it.
>
> —Hebrews 12:14-25

1. Peace should be pursued in relationships with other Christians. Do you have a present relationship situation in which you should attempt to pursue peace? ______________

   ____

   ____

2. Describe your situation and provide ways in which you can pursue peace with an individual or group of individual believers. ______________________________

   ____

   ____

   ____

   ____

3. Getting you to take on a spirit of offense is a strategy the devil uses to destroy you. Describe how this spirit has operated against you in the past. How did the devil strategize to divide you from others and others from you? ______________

   ____

   ____

4. What is the primary weapon for battling a spirit of offense?

5. Have you ever felt offended by someone's subtle actions, which later turned out to be nothing? Describe the situation.

6. How did you handle your feelings of offense?

7. What would have been a better way to handle it?

8. Do you have a root of rejection in your life? Explain.

9. Are you harboring deep-seated offenses in your heart toward other Christians? Explain.

10. What is the Bible remedy for offenses?

11. Suppose you are a doctor, your church is the patient and strife is the disease. Write a prescription for your church using Galatians 5:14–15.

Dear Lord, I forgive everyone against whom I've harbored an offense. I ask You to forgive them for any sin they have committed against me and to restore my love and fellowship with them where possible. Strengthen my insecurities and help me to not be easily offended. Lord, I choose to walk as Christ did, loving freely and forgiving everyone. Give me a heart of love toward all my brothers and sisters in Christ, especially those who have mistreated me. In Jesus' name, amen.

Nine

How Strife Affects Your Health

Strife brings stress, and stress brings sickness. We are vessels created by God for righteousness, peace and joy. We were never created to house strife, worry, hatred, bitterness, resentment, unforgiveness, rage, anger, jealousy, turmoil and upset of every kind. Our bodies are built to endure a lot of punishment and still survive, but filling the temple full of wrong things does damage it.

Thousands and thousands of people are sick today. There are more and more sicknesses and diseases all the time. I believe that a lot of disease is caused by *dis-ease.* The symptoms and the sickness are real, but the root cause is stress. Our bodies eventually break down from stress.

The Result of Anger

Strife causes much of the stress in our lives. Nothing is physically harder on me than getting angry or upset—

especially if I stay that way for very long. No wonder the Bible tells us:

> When angry, do not sin; do not ever let your wrath (your exasperation, your fury or indignation) last until the sun goes down.
>
> —Ephesians 4:26

> Understand [this], my beloved brethren. Let every man be quick to hear [a ready listener], slow to speak, slow to take offense and to get angry.
>
> —James 1:19

In the early years of our marriage I would get angry and stay that way for days or, occasionally, weeks at a time. Being angry and upset seemed to make me more energetic for a while, but when the anger subsided, I felt as if someone had pulled the plug and drained all my energy.

Some people eat more when they are angry. It's a way to say, "I'll show you." Some eat to comfort themselves when they are hurting. I always lost my appetite when I was upset or angry. It's a good thing I did, or I would have been obese, because I was upset about something most of the time.

I felt sick much of the time. But I never connected my sick feelings to my anger—and I doubt that most people do. I had headaches, back trouble, colon trouble and tension in my neck and shoulders. The doctor ran tests but could not find anything wrong with me. He concluded it was probably stress. That angered me even more! I knew that I was sick, and as far as I was concerned, it wasn't stress causing the sickness.

I had always been a very intense person. I lived with great intensity. When I cleaned the house, I worked hard, and I got angry when anyone messed it up. I wanted a house to look at—not to live in. I knew how to work, but I did not know how to live.

I had strife with myself, with Dave, the children, family members, neighbors and even God. I did a fair job of hiding it from those I wished to impress, but my inner life was almost always in a turmoil. No matter how well we may hide things from other people, the damage is still going on in our physical bodies and minds if we live under continual stress.

The Results of Too Much Stress

Stress can be mental, emotional or physical tension, strain or distress. Stress was originally an engineering term. How much stress could be placed on the steel beams in the building structure without it collapsing? Today, more people are collapsing than buildings! We are built by God in a marvelous way. We are built to handle—and handle well—a normal amount of stress.

Everyone has some stress. If you go out of a warm house into the bitter cold, it creates thermal stress on your body. There is a certain amount of mental stress to each person's job. Our son, David, works for us in the ministry, and he has said how tired mentally he is when he arrives home from work in the evening. He has a job that requires a lot of thinking, and he needs time to rest his mind when he gets home.

We travel a lot in our ministry outreach, and I get tired. Often I speak at several meetings in one weekend. I come home tired. I am doing what God has called me to do, but it creates a normal amount of physical stress. Stress in each of these instances cannot be avoided, but we must realize that proper rest and quiet time are vital to rebuild the energies that have been expended.

No wonder God established that man should work six days and then have a Sabbath—one day in seven to totally rest from all his labors. (See Exodus 20:8–10.) Even God rested from His labors after six days of creation work. (See Genesis 2:2.)

We can handle normal stress, but when things get out of balance or excessive, we often sacrifice our good health. In today's world, more people feel bad than good. People are tired, worn out and weary. They have little or no energy. They cannot walk very far, and running is out of the question. Most are too tired to climb the steps, and a simple thing like a sink full of dirty dishes can throw someone into depression.

Medical science has come up with all kinds of names for this new batch of diseases, but I think the root of much of it is the lack of peace that Jesus encouraged us to live in.

The world itself is a stressful place. The noise levels are growing at an alarming rate. Years ago, you could pull up beside a car in traffic with its windows down and hear a restful or joyful song playing that would make you feel a little better. You might even exchange a smile or a wave of hello with that driver, even though you did not know him.

But today, the sounds booming out from many cars are stressful. The volume alone can make a sane person want to scream, and the music sounds like wild screaming from someone who has just witnessed a brutal scene. The sounds seem to be calling for the deepest rebellion hidden in men's souls.

Your smile or wave may bring accusations of ulterior motives. If you look too long at someone, that person may scream obscenities at you. Don't expect much courtesy on the roads, but do be careful of cars darting in front of you and cutting into traffic.

Everybody is in a hurry. The sad thing is that they are going nowhere, and they don't know it. All of this creates an atmosphere that is void of peace. The atmosphere in the world today is supercharged with strife and stress.

Many families are experiencing financial pressure. Normal living frequently requires two incomes, thus both parents in a home have to work, or maybe the dad works two jobs. Many single mothers work two or three jobs to pay the bills, and still have all the other work to run a household that must be done at night.

Satan-Induced Stress

Tired people succumb to temptation easier than rested ones. Tired people get angry quicker. They are more impatient and more easily frustrated. It doesn't take a genius to recognize the plan of Satan. Remember, he plots and plans and lays schemes. He plans your destruction, and he works his plan in deceptive ways that you may not recognize at first.

I experienced a lot of stress in the early days of my own ministry. I felt the weight of responsibility on my shoulders. I thought about the potential problems almost constantly. Where would the money come from? How could I get speaking engagements when nobody knew who I was? How could I get on radio stations? I lived in fear and human reasoning—I lived in stress. The stress often caused strife between Dave and me.

Mainly, I was in strife with my circumstances. I could not seem to get things to move along as quickly as I wanted them to. I had a vision, and it was not progressing in my timing. I tried one thing first, and then another, but all to no avail.

I would let some of my stress out in front of Dave and my children. I hid it from those involved in ministry with me or from those I needed to impress with my *great* faith. I have since learned living in faith means entering into God's rest. (See Hebrews 4:3.)

But hiding my feelings did not prevent damage. I found myself in the doctor's office frequently. He continued to tell me I was under stress. Several different doctors all told me, "Young lady, you do not realize how stressful your job is."

They told me, but I did not believe them. I knew God had called me to be in full-time ministry, but I still had to learn to do it peacefully. My body was paying the price. I was under stress and it was making me sick. Today I can see clearly that what the doctors told me was accurate.

We cannot live in the world with other people and not have some stress. The question is not, "Do you have stress?" Everybody does. But the question is, "Are you managing stress? Are you taking measures to avoid more than you can manage? Are you resting, eating right, laughing enough and casting your care on God? Are you out of balance? Living in extremes? How often do you get angry? How long do you stay angry?"

Our Body's Response to Stress

Each time you get upset, each time your emotions rise to the boiling point, your internal organs have to work harder to accommodate the strain. They will only last for a certain period of time, and when they begin to wear out, they will start showing signs of the strain they have been under.

Let me share with you what your body goes through internally each time you get upset. I am not a doctor, but in my own terms, I will try to explain what happens. The onset of stress sets off an alarm in our body to defend itself from threatening events. Even thinking of an upsetting event or imagining danger can set off the alarm. A chain of internal responses are set into motion, and we are prepared to fight the danger or run from it. This is called fight or flight.

The stressor (the thing which is causing stress) sends a message to your brain through the pituitary gland and nervous system. Your brain sends the alarm message on to your adrenal gland, which releases hormones such as adrenaline, increasing your heart rate, raising blood pressure, sending glucose to your muscles and raising cholesterol. The threat of stress sets in motion a complex chain of responses to prepare us for "fight or flight"—either to attack what is threatening us or to run away from it.[1]

The body says to the organs, "I am under attack! Help me fight this, or help me get away from it. I need extra strength and energy to help me in this emergency!" The body organs begin to help. They are equipped to handle emergencies. But when a person lives in a perpetual state of emergency, the organs wear out.

The time comes when the organs are exhausted from trying to handle all the emergencies, and they find they can no longer handle even normal stress. Suddenly, something snaps! For some people, it is their minds. For others, it affects the emotions. For many others, physical health is affected.

Here is an example of what happens. Take a rubber band and stretch it out as far as you can. Then, let it relax. Do this over and over. After a while, you will find that the rubber band loses its elasticity. It becomes limp. Keep the process up long enough, and finally, one stretch too many, it snaps. This is what happens to us if we keep stretching ourselves too far too many times.

Finally, sickness arrives. People say, "I don't know what's wrong, but I just don't feel good." They have headaches, backaches, neck and shoulder pain, strain, stomach ulcers, colon problems and other ailments. When they tell the doctor how they feel, he calls it "adrenal weakness" or a "virus" of one sort or another.

In many instances the root cause is years of strife-filled, stressful living. Stress causes illness by destroying the body's immunological defense system. The individual's body cannot fight off germs and infection. The organs just plain wear out. Then the individual "feels" exhausted.

Live Positively

Negative thoughts, words and emotions cause stress, and stress can cause sickness. Positive thoughts, words and emotions bring health and healing. Consider the following five scriptures:

1. "A calm and undisturbed mind and heart are the life and health of the body, but envy, jealousy, and wrath are like rottenness of the bones" (Prov. 14:30).

Wrath is violent, resentful anger or rage. To be wrathful means to be very angry. Such upset causes sickness because the emotional turmoil eats away at good health and a sound body. A calm and peaceful mind ministers health to the entire being.

2. "My son, attend to my words; consent and submit to my sayings. Let them not depart from your sight; keep them in the center of your heart. For they are life to those who find them, healing and health to all their flesh" (Prov. 4:20–22).

What brings and ministers healing and health? Meditating on God's Word and not on the things that cause stress. Jesus is our peace. He is also the living Word. When we abide in the Word, peace is abundant. It flows like a river.

3. "Lean on, trust in, and be confident in the Lord with all your heart and mind and do not rely on your own understanding. In all your ways know, recognize, and acknowledge Him, and He will direct and make straight and plain your paths. Be not wise in your own eyes; reverently fear and worship the Lord and turn [entirely] away from evil. It shall be health to your nerves and sinews, and marrow and moistening to your bones" (Prov. 3:5–8).

When the mind is calm, health is protected. The wise man trusts in God rather than worrying. I spent years reasoning and trying to figure everything out, and it affected my health adversely. I feel much better physically now than I did when I was thirty-five. Why? I don't worry now. I have learned to cast my care upon God so that I don't live under constant pressure.

Learning to cast my care has also prevented strife between Dave and me. In the past, I would keep pushing, trying to get Dave to see things my way. Now I back off and ask God to change what needs to be changed.

4. "There are those who speak rashly, like the piercing of a sword, but the tongue of the wise brings healing" (Prov. 12:18).

Speaking rashly often starts arguments. The phrase "piercing of a sword" is descriptive of hurtful words that stab and wound. But a wise man can use his mouth to bring healing. Have your mouth full of the Word of God, not your own words. Your health will improve! I know because mine did.

5. "A happy heart is good medicine and a cheerful mind works healing, but a broken spirit dries up the bones" (Prov. 17:22).

How much plainer could it be said? A person who is happy, light-hearted and cheerful will be healthy. An angry person is neither cheerful nor happy, and, very likely, not healthy either.

Jesus gave us the answer to life's potential stressors. He said:

> I want you to have perfect peace and confidence. In the world you have tribulation and trials and distress and frustration; but be of good cheer, For I have overcome the world. [I have deprived it of power to harm you and have conquered it for you.]
>
> —JOHN 16:33, AUTHOR'S PARAPHRASE

The stress of traffic, job, children or relationships has no power to harm you if you remain calm and cheerful.

Certainly Jesus would not leave us in a world that had the power to make us sick without giving us a solution. The stress is in the world, but He is in us.

> Greater is he that is in you, than he that is in the world.
>
> —1 John 4:4, kjv

But the stress in the world is not the only stress that can affect the believer. Sometimes the source of our stress is within—we have strife within ourselves.

LIFE WITHOUT STRIFE

STUDY QUESTIONS

CHAPTER 9
HOW STRIFE AFFECTS YOUR HEALTH

Stress was originally an engineering term used when determining how much pressure steel beams or other structural features could endure before they began to buckle and finally collapse. Unresolved anger and other forms of strife produce the same effect upon your body.

Here's what the Bible says about anger:

> When angry, do not sin; do not ever let your wrath (your exasperation, your fury or indignation) last until the sun goes down.
>
> —EPHESIANS 4:26

> Understand [this], my beloved brethren. Let every man be quick to hear [a ready listener], slow to speak, slow to take offense and to get angry.
>
> —JAMES 1:19

1. Using Ephesians 4:26 and James 1:19, write a biblical response to your anger. ______________________________

____

____

2. What stress factors are you dealing with in your life at the present time? ______________________________

____

____

____

3. Living in faith means entering into God's rest according to Hebrews 4:3. Apply this truth to the stress factors in your own life. ______________________________

____

____

____

4. Mediating on the Word of God brings health and healing to your body. Using Proverbs 4:20–22, describe how you can walk in good health, free from stress-induced sickness. ______

______

______

5. Apply Proverbs 14:30 to your temper. ______

______

______

6. How do your words impact your health? ______

______

7. Recall a situation in which your words fueled a stressful situation. ______

______

______

8. What should you have done in that situation to reduce the level of stress? ______

______

______

9. Happiness and health are directly linked according to Proverbs 17:22. Using 1 John 4:4 from the King James Version, write a new commitment to live a happier, less stressful life. ______

______

______

Dear heavenly Father, please give me the grace I need to live in a stress-filled world. Help me to speak words that produce peace in my own mind and body and in the lives of others. Help me to obey Your admonition never to let the sun go down on my anger. I surrender my thoughts, words, attitudes and health to You. Amen.

Ten

Are You in Strife With Yourself?

The Bible is a book about relationships. It seems to major on three specific relationships: our relationship with God, with ourselves and with our fellowman. Several years ago, I was at a time in my life when I was seeking to walk in peace. I no longer wanted only to hear about peace, but I was determined to find out how to enjoy a peaceful life. It is not possible to enjoy life without peace. One day I read the following scripture:

> For let him who wants to enjoy life and see good days [good—whether apparent or not] keep his tongue free from evil and his lips from guile (treachery, deceit). Let him turn away from wickedness and shun it, and let him do right. Let him search for peace (harmony; undisturbedness from fears, agitating passions, and moral conflicts) and seek it eagerly. [Do not merely desire peaceful relations with God, with your

> fellowmen, and with yourself, but pursue, go after them!]
>
> —1 Peter 3:10-11

I still enjoy just reading over this passage and soaking up the power from its principles for successful daily living. It gives four specific principles for the person who desires to enjoy life.

1. Keep your tongue free from evil.
2. Turn away from wickedness.
3. Do right.
4. Search for peace.

1. Keep your tongue free from evil.

God's Word states clearly that the power of life and death is in the mouth. I can bring blessing or misery into my life with my words. I must choose my words carefully if I want to enjoy my life.

2. Turn away from wickedness.

We must take action to remove ourselves from wickedness or from a wicked environment. The first chapter of Psalms instructs us to avoid sitting inactively in the pathway of sinners. The action we must take could mean altering our friendships and eating lunch alone instead of sitting in the middle of office gossip. It could even mean loneliness for a period of time. New beginnings require endings. The desire to have a new life—one filled with righteousness, peace and joy—will require the death of some things as we wait on God to give birth to new ones.

3. Do right.

The decision to do right must follow the decision to stop doing wrong. It may appear that the one automatically follows the other, but it doesn't. Both are definite choices.

Repentance is twofold; it requires turning away from sin and turning to righteousness. Some people turn from their sin, but they never make the decision to start doing right. As a result, they are lured back into sin.

The Bible is filled with the following "positive replacement principle":

> Rejecting all falsity and being done now with it, let everyone express the truth with his neighbor . . . Let the thief steal no more, but rather let him be industrious, making an honest living with his own hands.
>
> —Ephesians 4:25, 28

4. Search for peace.

"Let him search for peace" is the fourth instruction to the man who truly desires to enjoy his life (1 Pet. 3:11). Notice that we must search for it, pursue it and go after it. We cannot merely desire peace without any accompanying action, but we must desire peace with action. In our search for peace, remember the three specific relationships we need to consider: our relationship with God, with ourselves and with our fellowman.

Are you at peace with yourself? Most individuals are in strife with themselves. Since we spend more time with ourselves than we do with anyone else, this becomes a major problem. As a matter of fact, you cannot get away from yourself! The person who does not get along with himself will probably not get along with others. If you cannot enjoy yourself, you won't enjoy other people either.

Learn to Accept Yourself

It is difficult to like and accept oneself. Self-rejection and self-hatred are two of the biggest problems people have to deal with. Many people have this problem and don't know it. I suffered from not liking myself for many years, but I thought the problem was caused by everyone else. I didn't enjoy many other people either, and I could sense that most of them did not enjoy me.

The way we see ourselves is the way others will see us. This is proven scripturally by the example in the Book of Numbers of the twelve spies sent by Moses to investigate the promised land. (See Numbers 13.) When the spies came back from scouting out the promised land, ten of the spies gave a very negative report.

> There we saw the Nephilim [or giants], the sons of Anak, who come from the giants; and *we were in our own sight as grasshoppers, and so we were in their sight.*
>
> —Numbers 13:33, emphasis added

I was not well-liked because I did not like myself. How can we expect others to accept us if we reject ourselves? We reap what we sow. (See Galatians 6:7.) This is a problem with many people. I believe a large percentage of all the problems people encounter is related to how they feel about themselves. Many people carry shame and reproach from the past, and it must be removed before victorious Christianity will emerge.

Why People Reject Themselves

The number one reason most people reject themselves is because of their weaknesses and mistakes. It would be easy to accept ourselves if we had no flaws. But we do have flaws. People reject themselves because they can't separate their "who" from their "do." What I *do* is not always perfect. But I still know *who* I am—a child of God whom He loves very much. My worth and value come from the fact that Jesus died for me—not because I do everything perfectly. (See Romans 3:22–23; 4:5.)

You have tremendous worth and value. You are special to God, and He has a good plan for your life. (See Jeremiah 29:11.) You have been purchased with the blood of Christ.

(See Acts 20:28.) The Bible refers to the "precious blood of Christ," indicating that Christ paid a high price indeed to ransom you and me (1 Pet. 1:19). Believe it, and you'll begin to receive it. The truth will bring healing to your soul and freedom to your life.

Many examples are given in God's Word of weak people who were chosen by God to accomplish great things for His glory. Don't rate yourself as unusable just because you have some weaknesses. God gives each of us the opportunity to be one of Jesus' successes. His strength is made perfect in our weakness. (See 2 Corinthians 12:9.) Our weakness gives Him the opportunity to show His power and His glory.

Instead of wearing yourself out trying to get rid of your weakness, give it to Jesus. He can make it disappear, or He can fill it with His strength. Both are equal as far as I am concerned.

The disciples were ordinary men who possessed weaknesses just like you and I. The Gospels clearly imply that Peter was a rugged and volatile fisherman—often displaying impatience, anger and rage. In one crucial moment, so fearful that he would be discovered to be a disciple of Jesus, he succumbed to an act of denial that labeled him "coward" for a chapter of history.

Andrew may have seemed softhearted and too kindly to be anything more than a follower. He avoided the role of leader, being willing to play "second fiddle" to his brother, Simon Peter, and his boisterous, competitive friends, James and John.

James and John are remembered for little beyond the fact that their mother sought positions of equality for them at Jesus' side when He established His kingdom. Could it be they were a bit too ambitious?

Thomas was a man afraid to place his trust in his leader. Everything had to be proven to him before he could accept it.

And then there was Matthew. The religious leaders of the day were outraged that Jesus would even consider socializing with this lowly tax collector. Imagine their horror when Jesus dined with him at his home and invited him to become one of His followers and close associates.

Probably the only man the religious leaders of that day would have considered worthy of any admiration at all was Judas. To the world's eye, Judas had business strengths and personality qualities that spelled success. But his greatest natural strengths became his greatest weaknesses—and brought destruction into his life.

See Weakness As Jesus Sees It

I find it interesting that those whom the world recommended, Jesus rejected. And those whom the world rejected, Jesus said, in essence, "Give them to Me. I don't care how many faults they have. If they will trust Me, I can do great and mighty things through them."

Jesus prayed all night before selecting the twelve men who became His close companions for three years. They had multiple weaknesses, and He knew it when He invited them into relationship with Him. Yet, with the exception of Judas Iscariot, they carried on Jesus' ministry in a dynamic way after His death, resurrection and ascension.

First Corinthians 1:25–29 unveils the heart of God toward those with weakness.

> The foolish thing [that has its source in] God is wiser than men, and the weak thing [that springs] from God is stronger than men. For [simply] consider your own call, brethren; not many [of you were considered to be] wise according to human estimates and standards, not many influential and powerful, not many of high and noble birth.
>
> [No] for God selected (deliberately chose) what in the world is foolish to put the wise to shame, and what

> the world calls weak to put the strong to shame. And God also selected (deliberately chose) what in the world is low-born and insignificant and branded and treated with contempt, even the things that are nothing, that He might depose and bring to nothing the things that are, so that no mortal man should [have pretense for glorying and] boast in the presence of God.

Wow! These scriptures give me such hope for my future. God can use even me! And God can use you! I encourage you to get your eyes off what you think is wrong with you and look to Jesus. Draw strength from His boundless might. Let His strength fill up your weaknesses. We are equal in Christ. For example, one person may have a measure of 10 percent weakness and 90 percent strength. Another person's measure is 40 percent weakness and 60 percent strength. In the natural way of speaking we would say the second person is weaker than the first and, therefore, less desirable for any given task.

But God does not see and judge as man does. Both of these individuals are equal to Christ, simply because He is willing to supply the added measure of strength to each individual. Thus, in Christ, they are both operating at the same level or capacity.

This is a marvelous biblical truth, and it sets us free to be all we can be—without fear of rejection and without having to fear our inherent weaknesses. If you grasp this truth, you will never need to be in strife with yourself again!

I was at war with Joyce for many years. I did not like myself, and tried to change myself continually. The more I struggled to change, the more frustrated I became, until the glorious day when I discovered Jesus accepted me just as I was. He, and only He, could get me to where I needed to be. No amount of struggle or self-effort could perfect the flaws in me. It is accomplished "Not by might, nor by power, but by my spirit saith the LORD of hosts" (Zech. 4:6, KJV).

Recently, a woman told me how she had been delivered from a spirit of strife after one of our seminars. "I had so much strife in my life that there was not one area or relationship that was not strife-filled and strife-controlled," she said. She heard people speak of "the peace that passes understanding," but she never understood what they meant. She said that she felt different after the seminar.

However, after attending the teaching sessions where I exposed the spirit of strife, she experienced peace for the first time in her life. The peace was so prevalent that when she awoke the next morning, she was not even sure how to go about getting out of bed. She literally had to relearn some of the simplest things in life.

That was due to the fact that everything she did was motivated by and done with strife. She was continually judging, criticizing and being disappointed with herself. Rejecting herself, she rejected all the abilities God had given her. She felt terrible about herself, so she strived constantly to be better. She had contempt for all her faults and weaknesses, and had never been able to see her strengths.

You see, we have some of both—strengths and weaknesses. The apostle Paul testified:

> I will all the more gladly glory in my weaknesses and infirmities, that the strength and power of Christ (the Messiah) may rest (yes, may pitch a tent over and dwell) upon me!
>
> —2 Corinthians 12:9

He wrestled with his weaknesses, but he learned that Christ's strength and grace would be sufficient.

Know Where to Lean

In other words, God was saying, "Paul, I really don't have to get rid of the problem, and you do not have to worry about it. I will fill it up with My strength, and it will be the same as if it was gone—*as long as you lean on Me!"*

Now we see our real problem. We are independent and don't like the idea of leaning on anyone continually. In my natural personality, I tend to be harsh in my dealings with people, especially if someone has irritated me, and I am feeling rather impatient. We know that this is not a good trait in a minister.

For years I tried to be gentle. I would determine, resolve and exercise all the self-control I could muster. Although I did improve, there were still those awful moments when the real me emerged. After years of wondering, How can God ever use me? How can He trust me? What if I offend someone? God finally showed me that my constant victory was dependent on my constant abiding in and leaning on Him.

> I am the Vine; you are the branches. Whoever lives in Me and I in him bears much (abundant) fruit. However, apart from Me [cut off from vital union with Me] you can do nothing.
>
> —JOHN 15:5

> Dwell in Me, and I will dwell in you. [Live in Me, and I will live in you.] Just as no branch can bear fruit of itself without abiding in (being vitally united to) the vine, neither can you bear fruit unless you abide in Me.
>
> —JOHN 15:4

Knowing this truth forces me to lean on Him continually. My need drives me to seek His face. I cannot give Him glory unless I lean on Him. God does not need to lean on me—I need to lean on Him. He has called me to minister in His behalf. Because He called me, He filled me with desire to do it. Yet, I know my faults and weaknesses could prevent me from reaching my goal. For years I fought with the flaws, and I never moved beyond the place of fighting.

I am sure people have looked at me and said, "No way! God can't be calling you to do anything major." I wanted to believe God and to believe what my heart was telling me, but I heard the voices of people and let their opinions affect me.

I listened to the devil, who gave me a running daily inventory of all my flaws and inabilities. He reminded me how often I tried to change and failed. But then the light of Romans 7:24–25 reached me.

> O unhappy and pitiable and wretched man that I am! Who will release and deliver me from [the shackles of] this body of death? O thank God! [He will!] through Jesus Christ (the Anointed One) our Lord!

Finally I was able, by God's grace, to believe that He chose me on purpose. I was not "pushed off on the Lord as a last resort" after He had tried to get two hundred others. *He chose me!* He deliberately chooses those the world would call weak and foolish, and He does it to confound the wise. (See 1 Corinthians 1:27.)

Make a decision today to get out of strife with yourself. Come to terms with yourself. Learn to laugh at yourself a little. Don't be so intense. God leaves imperfections in even the choicest of His saints to assure they will always need to lean on Him.

God often uncovers something to me about myself which He keeps hidden from others. I may feel I am awful, but others think I am wonderful. Oh, how marvelous our God truly is! He can uncover and hide at the same time. He shows me my flaws to keep me humble. He hides them from others so they cannot find fault with me. I belong to God. My flaws are God's business—and God's alone.

Beware of Judging One Another

If a neighbor came to my door complaining about the way my son styles his hair, I would tell him (hopefully politely) to mind his own business. My child is not his affair. This is the same protective attitude that our heavenly Father has over His children. Satan is "the accuser of our brethren" (Rev. 12:10), but he is also a liar. (See John 8:44.)

We are not to pass judgment on each other.

> Who are you to pass judgment on and censure another's household servant? It is before his own master that he stands or falls. And he shall stand and be upheld, for the Master (the Lord) is mighty to support him and make him stand.
>
> —Romans 14:4

I stand because Jesus holds me up. When a child is learning to walk, the parent is always close by, holding his hand and helping him keep his balance so he does not fall and hurt himself. I stand because my Father supports me and holds me up! I am upheld by His power, not my own!

Are you in strife with yourself due to other people's judgments and opinions? Look at Paul's comment concerning the criticism of others.

> But [as for me personally] it matters very little to me that I should be put on trial by you [on this point], and that you or any other human tribunal should investigate and question and cross-question me. I do not even put myself on trial and judge myself.
>
> —1 Corinthians 4:3

Some people were judging Paul's faithfulness. He did not try to defend himself, nor did he become angry. He simply said, "I do not care what you think. I do not even judge myself." Many times in the past, I have opened to this passage and soaked it in, trusting the power of God's Word to deliver me from self-judgment and criticism.

You cannot conquer the enemy, but God's Word can. Trust

the Word to deliver you, not yourself. Go to the Word when you are in trouble. When temptation comes knocking at your door, answer with the Word.

Why is it so important that people get out of strife with themselves? We cannot move into peace until we have first been established in righteousness. The kingdom of God is righteousness, peace and joy in the Holy Ghost. (See Romans 14:17.) This kingdom principle shows me a progression. If I desire joy, I must have peace, and to have peace I must have righteousness—a functioning reality of righteousness, not just a confession of righteousness.

Confess Righteousness

We start with a confession of righteousness. We call the things that are non-existent as though they already were. (See Romans 4:17.) That is our privilege as children of God. He also speaks of the non-existent as if it were. God told Abram He had made him the father of many nations long before Abram had a child to be his heir. God spoke of it as if it already existed, and we have the same privilege.

I can say I am the righteousness of God in Christ because the Word says that I am. (See 2 Corinthians 5:21.) The more I do say it, the stronger the reality of it grows in me. But to move on to real peace, I need righteousness established as truth in my soul. I must know that I know that I know. It must be so established in my heart that the "accuser of our brethren" (Rev. 12:10) cannot steal it from me with his lies.

I must be so established in righteousness through the blood of Christ, that even looking at my flaws does not defeat me. Abraham "did not weaken in faith when he considered the [utter] impotence of his own body which was about as good as dead because he was about a hundred years old, or [when he considered] the barrenness of Sarah's [deadened] womb" (Rom. 4:19).

He looked at his flaws and was not moved in the least. Abraham believed God, and it was counted to him as righteousness. I am righteous—not because I never make a mistake, but because Jesus never made one. He is the Perfect One, and my faith in Him causes the Father to view me as righteous also. You and I can eliminate all strife with ourselves and move into that blessed peace that leads to a joy-filled life. Jesus purchased that life for us by His death and resurrection.

CHAPTER 10
ARE YOU IN STRIFE WITH YOURSELF?

Are you pursuing peace with yourself? The Bible says:

> For let him who wants to enjoy life and see good days [good—whether apparent or not] keep his tongue free from evil and his lips from guile (treachery, deceit). Let him turn away from wickedness and shun it, and let him do right. Let him search for peace (harmony; undisturbedness from fears, agitating passions, and moral conflicts) and seek it eagerly. [Do not merely desire peaceful relations with God, with your fellowmen, and with yourself, but pursue, go after them!]
>
> —1 PETER 3:10–11

1. Based upon this verse, outline four basic principles for an individual who desires to enjoy life.

   ❑ ____________________

   ❑ ____________________

   ❑ ____________________

   ❑ ____________________

2. According Psalm 1:1, removing oneself from a negative environment is sometimes necessary for finding freedom from strife. For some, it might mean eating alone instead of surrounding yourself with office gossip. Are there ways in which you need to change your environment? ____________________

   ____

   ____

   ____

3. Choosing to do right takes a bold decision. Look up Ephesians 4:25, 28. In what ways will you begin displaying godly behaviors where you have previously fallen short? ____________________

   ____

   ____

   ____

LIFE WITHOUT STRIFE

Study Questions

4. Are you at peace with yourself? According to 1 Peter 3:11, if we desire peace we must search for it. How have you not searched for peace in relationship to yourself?__________

____

5. Do you accept yourself? What aspects of your "self" have you never accepted?____________________________

____

6. Read Number 13:33. This verse indicates that the way we see ourselves is the way others will end up seeing us. In what negative ways do you see yourself?______________

____

7. According to Romans 3:22–23 and Romans 4:5, write why Jesus Christ accepts you for who you are. ______________

____

8. What weaknesses do you have that you cannot feel good about?____________________________________

____

9. According to 1 Corinthians 1:25–29, describe how God feels about your weaknesses.____________________

____

10. Do you feel condemned by others who have judged you? Rewrite Paul's words from 1 Corinthians 4:3 about yourself regarding this situation.________________________

____

Dear Lord, I choose to accept myself as I am. I thank You for making me the person I am, with all my imperfections and flaws. Father, be my strength where I am weak, and give me the grace I need to accept myself the way You accept me. Thank You for loving me with supernatural love. Help me to see myself and my life through Your eyes. Amen.

Eleven

Strife With God

We have talked about the importance of being at peace with yourself. Now I want to share with you the importance of not being in strife with God. It may sound strange to you, but many people are mad at God for various reasons. God is not the source of anyone's problems. He is the *only* One who can help us!

Look again at the foundational principles in 1 Peter 3:10–11.

> For let him who wants to enjoy life and see good days [good—whether apparent or not] keep his tongue free from evil and his lips from guile (treachery, deceit). Let him turn away from wickedness and shun it, and let him do right. Let him search for peace (harmony; undisturbedness from fears, agitating passions, and moral conflicts) and seek it eagerly. [Do not merely desire peaceful relations with God, with your

> fellowmen, and with yourself, but pursue, go after them!]
>
> —1 Peter 3:10–11

Are You Angry at God?

Why do people fall into this trap? I was shocked when the Lord placed it upon my heart to minister to people in meetings along these lines. I didn't believe there would be many people who needed ministry concerning being angry at God, but I was wrong. A hidden rift with God is a root cause of many emotional problems. It is the cause of bitterness and a sour attitude toward life that opens the door to every kind of misery and torment.

Man is created to receive love from God, to enjoy and bask in it. He is to give love back to God lavishly, as well as to the world around him. God designed man for relationship with Himself—warm, tender, loving, open fellowship. Anytime this is missing, or hindered in any way, man suffers.

The Problem of Guilt and Condemnation

If a person withdraws from fellowship with God because of guilt and condemnation over his own sins and weaknesses, that person places himself in a position of continual misery. He cuts off the only source of power to help him. God, through Christ, is my helper when I sin. His grace will swallow up my sin if I believe it and receive it. He is the One who can strengthen me no matter what my weakness is. Since only God can help me, it is utter foolishness to cut myself off from Him.

The worst thing a person can do when he has trouble in his life is to blame the trouble on God. God wants to help us! He is not the troublemaker—the devil is. It is the world, the flesh and the devil that give us trouble—not God!

That is not to say that God will never lead us in a way that we would rather not go—because He does. The Israelites would have preferred a shorter route to the Promised Land. But God had a purpose in the way He led.

> When Pharaoh let the people go, God led them not by way of the land of the Philistines, although that was nearer; for God said, Lest the people change their purpose when they see war and return to Egypt. But God led the people around by way of the wilderness toward the Red Sea. And the Israelites went up marshaled [in ranks] out of the land of Egypt.
>
> —Exodus 13:17–18

God knows what is best for us. There are times when we feel, think or desire a certain path. We are tempted to get angry with God when He leads us a different way. Make a decision to trust God to know what is best for you. God is your friend—your best friend. You will never have another friend like Jesus.

Disappointment with life, with people or with circumstances can develop into disappointment with God. This is exactly what the devil wants! If you are angry at God, bitter or resentful toward God, He is giving you an opportunity as you read this book to be delivered from the trap that Satan set for you. God is your helper—not your enemy.

What about all the hard things that happen in our lives? I do not have a total answer to all of life's disappointments. In my own life, if I try to reason everything out, I become very confused. Confusion is not from God, so I have made a decision not to live in reasoning.

Fifteen years of my childhood—from age three through age eighteen—were filled with sexual abuse that brought emotional pain of the worst kind. I spent the next thirty years or more trying to overcome the first eighteen years. I was bitter toward life and people. I resented people who had nice lives and had not endured the agony I had. I did not know how to receive the love, grace and mercy of God that I needed.

But, I was spared the torment of being mad at God. Many people who have been abused do get mad at God. They cannot understand why God didn't help them. They cannot trust Him.

I can understand how that could happen. I was filled with questions. Why would a loving God sit by and watch a child suffer so terribly? Why didn't He stop the pain? We know that God can do anything He wants. We don't understand why He doesn't prevent the things that hurt us.

God gave me some answers to satisfy my questions, but I still have to comfort myself with the truth that we only "know in part" (1 Cor. 13:12). With our finite minds, we cannot understand cancer, loved ones snatched from us by death, abuse, drugs, alcohol, war and many other things that usher in pain that is almost unbearable. Our comfort must come from trusting God.

Sin and evil are in the world. The age-old battle between the forces of good and evil is still raging, and I suspect it will until the end of time. At times it appears that evil has won over good, but ultimate victory belongs to those who will put their trust in God.

Avoid Strife With God

Job was a man who trusted God. Yet when his faith was tried in the fiery furnace of affliction, he asked the same questions we ask.

> I loathe my life; I would not live forever. Let me alone, for my days are a breath (futility). What is man that You should magnify him and think him important? And that You should set Your mind upon him? And that You

should visit him every morning and try him every moment?

How long will Your [plaguing] glance not look away from me, nor You let me alone till I swallow my spittle? If I have sinned, what [harm] have I done You, O You Watcher and Keeper of men? Why have You set me as a mark for You, so that I am a burden to myself [and You]? And why do You not pardon my transgression and take away my iniquity? For now shall I lie down in the dust; and [even if] You will seek me diligently, [it will be too late, for] I shall not be.

—Job 7:16–21

Job was negative and discouraged. He questioned God and wanted to die because he was hurting so badly. He was confused because God had not delivered him yet. But we must read the end of the story.

And the Lord turned the captivity of Job and restored his fortunes, when he prayed for his friends; also the Lord gave Job twice as much as he had before.

—Job 42:10

When Job gave up his anger toward God and man, his breakthrough came. The psalmist experienced the same thing! Read the progression of his feelings.

Behold, these are the ungodly, who always prosper and are at ease in the world; they increase in riches. Surely then in vain have I cleansed my heart and washed my hands in innocency. For all the day long have I been smitten and plagued, and chastened every morning.

Had I spoken thus [and given expression to my feelings], I would have been untrue and have dealt treacherously against the generation of Your children. But when I considered how to understand this, it was too great an

> effort for me and too painful until I went into the sanctuary of God; then I understood [for I considered] their end.
>
> [After all] You do set the [wicked] in slippery places; You cast them down to ruin and destruction. How they become a desolation in a moment! They are utterly consumed with terrors! As a dream [which seems real] until one awakens, so, O Lord, when You arouse Yourself [to take note of the wicked], You will despise their outward show.
>
> For my heart was grieved, embittered, and in a state of ferment, and I was pricked in my heart [as with the sharp fang of an adder]. So foolish, stupid, and brutish was I, and ignorant; I was like a beast before You. Nevertheless I am continually with You; You do hold my right hand. You will guide me with Your counsel, and afterward receive me to honor and glory. Whom have I in heaven but You? And I have no delight or desire on earth besides You. My flesh and my heart may fail, but God is the Rock and firm Strength of my heart and my Portion forever.
>
> For behold, those who are far from You shall perish; You will destroy all who are false to You and like [spiritual] harlots depart from You. But it is good for me to draw near to God; I have put my trust in the Lord God and made Him my refuge, that I may tell of all Your works.
>
> —Psalm 73:12–28

Now permit me to give you my paraphrase of these scriptures.

> God, it sure seems that the wicked prosper and do better than I do. I am trying to live a godly life, but it does not seem to be doing any good. It looks as if it's all in vain. I am having nothing but trouble, and when I try to understand it, the pain is too much for me. However, I have

> spent time with You, and I can understand that in the end the wicked come to ruin and destruction.
>
> My heart was grieved. I was bitter and in a state of upset. I was stupid, God, ignorant, and behaving like a beast. Now I see that You are continually with me. You hold my right hand. Whom do I have in heaven, God, but You? Who will help me? If You don't, there is no one on earth that can help me. You are my strength and my portion forever. It is good for me to trust in You, O Lord, and make You my refuge.

There are many other examples in the Word of God of men and women who did not understand what was happening to them. They went through periods of questioning, doubting, blaming and even criticizing God. But they realized they were being foolish. They repented and turned back to trusting God instead of being angry with Him.

Forgiveness Stands Between Defeat and Victory

I encourage people who have been angry with God to go through the process of forgiving Him. He does not need our forgiveness. But we need to work through the process and verbalize forgiveness in order to have a release from the anger, bitterness and resentment in our hearts.

If we can complete this process of forgiveness, we can be restored to a life of peace, but if we fail to forgive God when we need to do so, we will remain in strife. That's what happened in the following situations after the death of loved ones. The two stories are similar, but the endings are very different.

Several years ago, a woman lost her husband to cancer. During the time he suffered with his illness, he was born again, filled with God's Spirit and became totally committed to the gospel. He made every effort to share his testimony with as many people as possible. The entire family expected the man to be healed supernaturally by God and live his life as a testimony to the healing power of God.

He had received prophecies that he would live and not die. His family stood in faith and spoke the Word. They did everything they were told to do by their spiritual leaders or by the man's doctors. Yet, the man died.

Although the woman went through much confusion, anger and disappointment, she was able to place her trust in God and come through victoriously. On the seventh anniversary of his death, I received a letter from her thanking Dave and me for being with her during that time. She was grateful for the Word of God that she had received from our ministry and from her home church.

She told me how much she loves the Lord today. He is her whole life. She enjoys serving Him in any way she can. She still misses her husband, but she is at peace and walks in victory.

On the other hand, her children have not fared so well. They kept some of the bitterness they felt when their father died. The confusion in their spirits has affected their spiritual progress. They have not turned away from God completely, but they did fall backward and have never recovered.

Anger and bitterness toward God will stop you in your tracks and refuse to allow you to go forward. It is a "spiritual roadblock"—perhaps stronger than any other. Why? Simply because anger closes the door to the only One who can help, heal, comfort or restore our emotions and lives.

Another couple, who had served God aggressively for many years, had several children. One of the children died suddenly, and the man became bitter toward God. I am sure his thoughts were something like this: *God, I have served You faithfully all these years, and I don't understand why You have let this happen. Why didn't You protect us? How could You let us down like this? We don't deserve this, God.*

These kind of thoughts continued until the man became so bitter and angry that it began to affect his life like a cancer.

Eventually, he divorced his wife and continued on in a life of sin—wanting nothing to do with God.

Choose Life

In every disappointment and disaster—and there are many in our lives—we must choose how we will respond. God's Word says, "I set before you life and death . . . choose life" (Deut. 30:19).

When a circumstance brings death into our lives—physically, spiritually or emotionally—the only sane solution is to choose life. If we don't choose life, death continues to spread until it steals our spiritual life, peace, joy, hope, health and personal relationships. Let me give you a practical example from my own life.

Several years ago I went to the doctor for my yearly physical checkup. Dave had been insisting I go, but I had resisted because I don't like to spend my time doing things like that. My appointment was on October 31—Halloween. I asked to put it off for a week, but Dave was adamant that I go that day. During the examination I had a mammogram.

The next day my doctor called to say he had seen something on the test that looked suspicious. He wanted me to come back for a biopsy. I did not want to do that either, but once again my husband insisted I get it checked out. I went in the hospital as an outpatient, fully expecting to hear that everything was fine. We prayed and believed God, asked several others to pray and went on our merry way.

I went shopping on Saturday of that week, simply going on with my life and having a good time in Jesus. I fully expected to receive a good report from the doctor. When I returned home from shopping, I found a note advising me to call the doctor immediately. When I called, he told me that I had a tumor of a very fast-growing type of cancer. He recommended immediate surgery to remove my breast. He said he could not take just the tumor because he wanted to be sure he would get it all because of the type of cancer it was.

We sought God and prayed. Although the easiest thing for me would have been to trust God and not have the recommended surgery, that did not seem to be the way God was leading. My entire family—my husband and all four of my children—as well as a handful of close friends, all agreed that I should have the surgery. I also felt the same way, even though I really would rather not have taken that route.

I was gripped by fear so strong it almost knocked me down at times. Negative thoughts came—temptation to doubt God's love for me. I was tempted to doubt His integrity and to doubt my own self. The devil wanted me to try and figure out the situation. What had I done wrong? Why had God let this happen? Did God let it happen, or had I opened a door for the devil?

The bombarding thoughts were attacks from hell. Each attack was designed to destroy my faith in God. I am very grateful I was rooted and grounded in Christ and in His Word and love for me. Being established in Christ is very valuable at times like this.

Please note that I said "established in Christ," not "established in ministry." I believe many who minister to others are not rooted and grounded in the very principles they teach. It is easy to tell someone else what to do in hard times; it is another thing entirely to do it yourself when the need arises.

I had to ask myself, "What would I tell someone else to do in this exact same situation?" I knew what I would tell them: "Trust God! Don't try to figure it out. Ask God to reveal to you anything He may want you to see, but if He shows you nothing, remain at peace and walk it out." I would say, "It will all work out for good in the end if you don't faint and give up. Be positive, give praise and continue to be a blessing to others."

God told me, "Joyce, do what you would tell someone else to do in the same situation."

What was the outcome? I did have the surgery. And it turned out to be God's timing that Dave had insisted I go to the doctor on October 31 and not another day later. We were in the process of switching health insurance companies. We were unaware of it, but the switch was to be made on November 1.

After November 1, our old insurance would be no good. We were able to call and keep the original insurance. But if we had not done that, the new insurance would not have covered any of the cost because it would have been a preexisting condition. The new insurance had a clause that excluded preexisting conditions for one year. Thank God for the leading of the Holy Spirit!

That was only one of the ways we experienced the power and presence of the Lord.

I recovered faster than my doctor could believe. I left the hospital and stopped at the shopping mall on the way home to get some clothing that would be suitable for my recovery. I preached the evening before I went into the hospital. Two weeks after the surgery, I was able to minister at an all-day Christmas banquet where I taught twice.

I never lost my joy. I never got confused. We walked it out step by step and trusted that God was in charge. When all the tests came back, the report stated: "No more cancer. No problem with lymph nodes. No radiation or chemotherapy needed." What a glorious relief! I spent the next year preparing for replacement surgery, but I did not miss any of my regularly scheduled meetings during that experience. I did everything I normally did, and God worked mightily.

God provided born-again, Spirit-filled doctors at every phase of surgery and recovery, including my surgeon, plastic surgeon, gynecologist and many of the nurses. I experienced a tremendous display of love from the body of Christ. I learned a new dependence upon God that is still a blessing in my life today.

I could have chosen the route of anger at God, but it would have ruined my ministry. I would not be doing anything I am privileged to do today, including writing this book.

I cannot answer why God allowed that experience to happen to me. I don't know why. I can only "know in part" (1 Cor. 13:12). I am grateful I don't have to reason out all the things in life that I don't understand. What a wonderful privilege it is to trust God.

That cancer in my body was a portion of death. I had an opportunity to choose more death by becoming angry with God, but His grace was there for me to choose life. As a result, my life is moving forward in God today.

Unfortunate things may come into a person's life. We don't have control over every circumstance, but we can control our reactions to the circumstances. I encourage you to choose life.

Don't allow death into your life because of bitterness about adultery, divorce, death, lack, childlessness, miscarriage or abuse. If you are stuck in a place of bitterness against God, His arms are open wide right now. Run to God—not away from Him.

I recall a man who lost his son to cancer. Bitterly, he asked God, "Where were You when my son died?"

The Lord replied, "The same place I was when Mine died."

God didn't give him a lengthy explanation, but the Lord's answer caused the man to close his mouth in humility. It is never our place to criticize God.

Someday we will know even as we are known. (See 1 Corinthians 13:12.) That promise can sustain our lives until we are ushered into the eternal peace and blessedness of God. It will also help us to avoid strife with our fellowman.

LIFE WITHOUT STRIFE

STUDY QUESTIONS

CHAPTER 11
STRIFE WITH GOD

Although we may deny it, many of us are angry at God. We were created to receive love from God and to respond with our love to Him. Yet the root of many of our emotional problems stems from hidden or repressed anger toward God. This anger is also the cause of a bitter attitude toward life.

Prayerfully ask the Holy Spirit to show you any hidden anger or hurt toward God you have buried deep inside.

1. Is a particular situation or event that was difficult for you to understand at the root of your anger? Explain. ________

   ____

   ____

2. Did you feel a sense of abandonment, loneliness, rejection, disappointment or grief? Explain what you felt and why.

   ____

   ____

3. Have you ever expected God to lead you along a certain path, but found that He led you in a completely different direction? Look up Exodus 13:17–18 and write about your experience of being re-routed by God. ________

   ____

   ____

   ____

   ____

   ____

4. God is your helper—not your enemy. Yet Satan will often attempt to twist your perception to cause you to reject the One who loves you the most. To keep from being deceived by the devil, it is often necessary to choose to believe in God's love—regardless of how the devil makes you feel. Are you willing make that choice today?

   ❑ Yes ❑ No

5. Guilt and condemnation can also create a rift between you and God. Ask God to reveal to you if you have a place of guilt or condemnation in your heart. If you do, repent for it immediately and ask God for His help to keep you from falling back into this sin. Write out your prayer of repentance and your request for help.

6. What if you really want to continue in your guilt-producing behavior? Many find certain behaviors difficult to let go of. The Bible says that God works in you both to will and to do His good pleasure. (See Philippians 2:13.) This means that He'll help you want to change. If this sounds like you, write out a prayer asking God to give you the desire to change.

7. Have you ever felt like David when he wrote Psalm 73:12–28, asking why the wicked always seem to prosper while the righteous suffer constant affliction and disappointment? If so, write your own psalm expressing your personal feelings regarding this matter.

8. If you have ever felt disappointment and bitterness toward God, even though He is not to blame, you may need to forgive Him. Write a prayer forgiving God for your disappointment.

____

____

____

____

____

9. In every disappointment and disaster—and we all experience many—we must choose how we will respond. God's Word says, "I set before you life and death . . . choose life" (Deut. 30:19). You may have felt that your faith has been violated, your heart has been broken and your life has been utterly shattered. You may feel deep down that God could have stopped the train before it wrecked, but He did not. Regardless of what you've suffered or experienced, you have a choice to make today. Write a bold declaration stating your decision.

____

____

____

____

____

Lord Jesus, I submit my life to You today, all over again. I don't understand all of the circumstances of my life, and perhaps I never will while I live on this earth. I know that faith is not proven when it's easy. Lord, even though it is hard to choose to trust You at times, even though I do not fully understand, I submit my life to You. I thank You for loving me and keeping me until that day when I'll fully know as I am fully known—just as the Bible says in 1 Corinthians 13:12.

Twelve

Strife With Your Fellowman

There is probably nothing more challenging than walking in peace with people. And yet, it is vitally important. Keeping strife out of personal relationships requires extreme willingness. We must learn to recognize strife in its beginning stages and be willing to resist the devil at the onset of his attack.

The devil tempts virtually every relationship with strife. We cannot avoid it. We must confront it, get it out in the open and talk about it, trying to come to some terms of peace.

Walking in peace is a primary goal of mine. It is more important than many people realize. It was obviously important to the kingdom of God, because Jesus talked about it frequently. There are some startling statements in the Word of God regarding the need of peace in relationships.

The Divorce Issue

We know from Scripture that God hates divorce. (See

Malachi 2:14–16.) We are to be united—not separated. And yet, look at these verses in Corinthians:

> And if any woman has an unbelieving husband and he consents to live with her, she should not leave or divorce him. For the unbelieving husband is set apart (separated, withdrawn from heathen contamination, and affiliated with the Christian people) by union with his consecrated (set-apart) wife, and the unbelieving wife is set apart and separated through union with her consecrated husband. Otherwise your children would be unclean (unblessed heathen, outside the Christian covenant), but as it is they are prepared for God [pure and clean]. But if the unbelieving partner [actually] leaves, let him do so; in such [cases the remaining] brother or sister is not morally bound. But God has called us to peace.
>
> —1 Corinthians 7:13–15

I think that is a startling statement! We know that the Lord does not desire for any marriage to end in divorce. Yet Paul, speaking with inspiration from God, says that if the unbelieving partner does not want the relationship, and he (or she) leaves, just let him go because it is very important that we live in peace.

We should do everything we possibly can to make a relationship work, and this is especially true in marriage. But the bottom line is this: If a person absolutely does not want to be in relationship with you, but you keep trying to force it, it will never produce anything but strife. Please remember that strife opens the door for all kinds of other problems.

In the fifteenth chapter of Acts, we see that Paul and Barnabas had some difficulty in their ministry relationship.

> And after some time Paul said to Barnabas, Come, let us go back and again visit and help and minister to the

> brethren in every town where we made known the message of the Lord, and see how they are getting along.
>
> Now Barnabas wanted to take with them John called Mark [his near relative]. But Paul did not think it best to have along with them the one who had quit and deserted them in Pamphylia and had not gone on with them to the work. And there followed a sharp disagreement between them, so that they separated from each other, and Barnabas took Mark with him and sailed away to Cyprus.
>
> But Paul selected Silas and set out, being commended by the brethren to the grace (the favor and mercy) of the Lord. And he passed through Syria and Cilicia, establishing and strengthening the churches.
>
> —Acts 15:36-41

Paul and Barnabas were experiencing the same troubles in their relationship that people experience today. Barnabas wanted to give his relative, Mark, a job. Paul had already had an experience with Mark and felt it would not be wise. A "sharp" disagreement arose between them (v. 39).

Apparently, it was so sharp they knew they needed to get away from each other. It would have been much better if they could have resolved their differences and continued to work together, but since that was impossible, the next best thing to do was separate so they could live in peace.

I want to be very clear. I am not advocating that married couples separate if they find it difficult to get along. The Bible says if the "unbeliever" wants to depart—let him—because we are called to peace. Paul and Barnabas knew the importance of walking in peace, so they separated to make that possible. They were not two believers married to one another. They were two grown men trying to work together in ministry.

On the other hand, neither am I saying that a time of

separation might not be helpful in some specific marriage situations. A time of separation would be more desirable than a divorce. Perhaps during the separation both parties could see things more clearly. This frequently happens. People have time to clear their heads, let heated emotions cool down and get quiet enough to hear from the Lord. They have time to ask God what He wants them to do in their situation.

Sometimes we stare at a person's faults so long that we no longer can see his strengths. A time away from someone, even spending a week at a relative's house in another state, can help us see the good things about a person that we miss when he or she is always present. You know the old saying, "You never know what you have until you lose it."

Magnify the Positive

One of the best ways to turn around a sour relationship is to ignore the negatives and magnify the positive aspects of that person's character. Concentrating on the negative aspects of a relationship is one of the major causes of problems.

I love my husband very much. But there was a time in the early years of our marriage when I kept mental lists of every fault he ever displayed. I was a very negative person, and I literally searched for the faults and negative traits in people. I think I felt so bad about myself that it made me able to bear myself if I found plenty of things wrong with others.

Dave played golf every Saturday, and I hated it. I thought he was extremely selfish not to realize how hard it was for me to be home all week with the children, with no opportunity to go any place. We had only one car, and he drove it to work.

I felt trapped within the bounds of the three-block radius in which I was able to walk. However, within those three blocks were a bakery, a grocery store, a beauty salon and a dimestore (as they were called then). I was not spiritually intelligent enough to realize that God had blessed me with the convenience of having all those places available within walking distance.

I never considered that Dave worked all week, had loved sports all his life and that playing golf on Saturday was very important to him. I tried to get him to quit. I was angry almost every Saturday, and it only made him want to play more. The standards of the "law" only increase our problems; they cannot solve them. I tried to put him under law, and it made him want to stay away all the more.

In addition, I felt Dave did not talk to me enough, that he goofed around too much and he wasn't serious enough. I did not think he was aggressive enough either. I didn't agree with most of his opinions. The list of his faults went on and on.

In short, I hunted up everything negative and overlooked all his positive characteristics. I was so busy meditating on his faults and trying to correct them that I did not even realize what a blessing I had in my life.

When God finally taught me—after many years of misery—to magnify the good in life and people, it was amazing how many great qualities I discovered in my husband! Of course, those qualities were there all the time. I could have been enjoying him all those years. Are you majoring in someone's faults when you could be magnifying his good points?

I discovered that Dave was flexible and adaptable. He was, and is, very easy to get along with. He is not demanding at all. He is willing to eat almost anything. It does not matter to him if I feed him cold sandwiches or a hot meal. He allows me to buy anything for which we have enough money. Any time I want to invite people over to the house, it is fine with him. If I want to go out to dinner, that is fine. I can choose the restaurant.

Dave takes good care of himself physically. He looks much the same as he did when we married more than twenty-eight years ago, except older. The list of his good points is lengthy—longer than the list I kept of his negative qualities.

Be positive about the people with whom you have relationships. We all have faults, and if magnified, the faults become bigger than they really are. But when we magnify the good points in people, they become larger than the things that irritate us.

Today, if someone were to ask me what my husband's faults were, I would have to think hard to come up with some. Nobody is perfect, and Dave has some faults, but I don't pay much attention to them any longer, making them hard to remember.

If we sow mercy, we will reap mercy. (See Matthew 5:7.) Do you want mercy applied to your weaknesses and faults? The best way to insure obtaining mercy is to pay heed to the Word of God and sow mercy. Be plenteous in mercy.

I believe many divorces each year could have been prevented if the marriage partners had magnified each other's strong points. We should magnify strengths verbally to the individual as well as in our private thought life. When we edify and encourage people, we are helping him to be the best they can be. We pull the best out of them by magnifying the best.

Paul did this on a regular basis when he wrote to the various churches. Even when he corrected them, he also commended them for what they were doing right. He knew the art of correcting someone to get him to do his best without offending him. One example can be seen in the way he encouraged them to give.

> Now about the offering that is [to be made] for the saints (God's people in Jerusalem), it is quite superfluous that I should write you; for I am well acquainted with your willingness (your readiness and your eagerness to promote it) and I have proudly told about you to the people of Macedonia, saying that Achaia (most of Greece) has been prepared since last year for this contribution; and [consequently] your enthusiasm has stimulated the majority of them.

> Still, I am sending the brethren [on to you], lest our pride in you should be made an empty boast in this particular case, and so that you may be all ready, as I told them you would be; lest, if [any] Macedonians should come with me and find you unprepared [for this generosity], we, to say nothing of yourselves, be humiliated for our being so confident. That is why I thought it necessary to urge these brethren to go to you before I do and make arrangements in advance for this bountiful, promised gift of yours, so that it may be ready, not as an extortion [wrung out of you] but as a generous and willing gift.
>
> —2 CORINTHIANS 9:1–5

Paul encouraged them without sounding as if he was accusing or doubting them. He said he knew they were ready to give, and had been for a long time. He says he is proud of them, and that they will be a witness to other people. What a build-up he gives them before he tells them that he is sending someone to make sure their offering is prepared as planned.

Often, when ministers receive offerings, they approach it from a negative standpoint, talking as if they are trying to talk the people into doing something they don't want to do. I have been corrected by the Lord more than once for that same attitude when receiving offerings in my seminars. We must be positive and tell the people, "I believe you are ready to give and that you want to give. I believe you are generous people who love God and enjoy being part of the ministries that are helping you."

What a difference it would make in our lives if we could be totally positive. I am learning the power of being positive in everything. Let us be especially positive about the people in our lives. Look for and magnify the positive. It will help the other people improve, and it will help you enjoy them more right where they are. Being positive about another person will even help you to disagree agreeably when you have differing opinions.

LIFE WITHOUT STRIFE

Study Questions

Chapter 12
Strife With Your Fellowman

Walking in peace with others is often challenging. If possible, the devil will try to undermine every one of your relationships with strife. You cannot always avoid strife. Sometimes you must confront it, get it out in the open and try to come to some terms of peace.

The apostle Paul makes a powerful statement in 1 Corinthians 7:15: "God has called us to peace." It is not God's will or intention that we live at war with others. If peace is God's will for our lives, He will calm the storms of strife that rage against us and make peace possible.

1. List your relationships that have been attacked by strife.

   ____

   ____

   ____

2. It's possible that you are to blame—at least partially—for the strife in some of your relationships. However, it is also possible that you are being victimized by someone else's strife. Think carefully and prayerfully about the causes of strife in these relationships. Write down the hard-to-face truth you've discovered. ______________________________

   ____

   ____

   ____

3. First Corinthians 7:15 speaks about allowing an unbeliever to walk away from a marriage relationship rather than living in strife. God hates divorce. But He would actually have an unbelieving spouse walk away rather than force the believer to live in strife. This also relates to other relationships. Are you in any strife-filled relationships that you might be better off walking away from for the sake of peace—at least temporarily? ______________________________

   ____

   ____

4. Sometimes we look at a person's faults for so long that we no longer see his or her strengths. Is there a (non-marriage) relationship in your life that is at a similar breaking point? Spend time in prayer asking the Holy Spirit to give you insight on how to handle the division. Write about how you sense God is leading you to deal with this situation.

5. Magnifying the positive characteristics in a person is a good way to build relationship bridges. List some of the positive characteristics of a person with whom you've experienced strife.

Lord Jesus, please give me the grace to be gracious and positive in all my relationships. If some of my relationships are at the breaking point, show me how I might gain fresh perspective about the people involved. Help me to see the positive in everyone around me, and help me to speak in a positive manner, even when I must bring correction. Thank You, Lord.

Thirteen

How to Disagree Agreeably

Jesus is the King of Peace. We are joint heirs with Him, having the same Father. Therefore, I must be a peacemaker. If I am going to serve the Lord, I cannot live in strife. God did not merely suggest that we not be in strife—it is His command: "The servant of the Lord must not strive" (2 Tim. 2:24, KJV).

Everything God instructs us to do is for our good. It helps me follow through with obedience in difficult situations when I remember that, ultimately, doing it God's way will help me. Staying out of strife will require a continuing determined effort.

One of the reasons people have strife in their lives is because they are not determined enough to keep it out. Or, if they do resist it sometimes, they are not willing to do it all the time. I want to repeat myself to make sure that I have solidly made my point. Remember, staying out of strife is a continuing process.

> Blessed (enjoying enviable happiness, spiritually prosperous—with life-joy and satisfaction in God's favor and salvation, regardless of their outward conditions) are the makers and maintainers of peace, for they shall be called the sons of God!
>
> —MATTHEW 5:9

The King James version may be more familiar to you:

> Blessed are the peacemakers: for they shall be called the children of God.
>
> —MATTHEW 5:9

Being a peacemaker is a decision. The blessings are available to those who will be peacemakers, but not all are willing because it's not always easy. When you decide to be a peacemaker, does that mean you become a doormat for everyone just to keep peace? Does it mean that you can never give your opinion or let someone know how you feel about something? No! Emphatically no!

I have a strong, aggressive personality. I am also a verbal person. Over the years, my mouth has gotten me into a lot of trouble. Becoming a peacemaker was not easy for me. The abuse of childhood made me determined that nobody was going to take advantage of me as an adult.

I was busy taking care of myself. I was afraid if I did not stay in control of every situation that I would be taken advantage of and pushed around. When the Lord began teaching me about living in agreement, I had a very difficult time understanding how you could agree with someone with whom you had differing opinions.

Just keeping my mouth shut did not seem to be an option for me. The devil told me over and over, "If you do this, you will become a doormat for everyone in the world to walk on."

I'm sure that many of you have had the same "recording" played to you by the enemy. When I studied the Scriptures on submission and how a wife should submit and adapt to her husband, it was almost more than my flesh could take! But I finally grew to the point in my walk with God that I wanted to be submissive. I wanted to be a peacemaker. I wanted to keep the strife out of my life! I was seeking God seriously for a breakthrough in this area.

The devil then took advantage of my willing spirit and tried to get me out balance on the opposite extreme. While previously I had something to say about everything, after I desired to change, I felt I couldn't say anything at all. If Dave disagreed with me about something, I felt that "submission" meant that I could verbalize no further opinion. Otherwise, I would be in rebellion toward my husband.

This might not be a huge problem if you happen to be married to someone with whom you agree most of the time, but that was not the case with us. We have very different personalities, and we often see things from two totally different angles. Once people learn how to disagree agreeably, opposite viewpoints can be a very healthy experience. Being able to see a thing from several different perspectives brings the best conclusion.

While I would keep quiet outwardly, it was eating away at me inside. I was being quiet, but I was still in strife. Strife is "an angry undercurrent." I could only manage to stay quiet for a short period of time, and then I would explode.

When Dave and I sat down to talk about our problem, I realized that we had a communication problem. I came to understand that communication happens when all parties can express their hearts in a godly way. Communication is the number one problem in many relationships.

Many times, people try to discuss things but immediately end up arguing, causing strife. Over a period of years, they stop trying to communicate and major problems develop. This problem is the root of most divorces. Lack of proper communication may be the culprit behind most of the other (more obvious) problems in marriages. Even adultery can be caused by lack of proper communication.

In the early years of our marriage, I had a strong, overly aggressive personality. Dave was more passive and less inclined to confront me. After giving me some years to grow in God and partially overcome my past, the Holy Spirit began leading Dave to confront me more instead of just letting me have my way.

At first, my flesh nearly went crazy. I would get so upset that I felt like I wanted to run from the whole thing. Down deep inside I knew what God was trying to do, and one part of me sincerely wanted Him to do it, but another part of me (my flesh) wanted to scream and run.

As Dave continued to press on and confront me, we had to learn how to communicate properly. We both had things to learn. He had not confronted me for years, and when he started to do so, he came on too strong. I was not accustomed to being confronted at all, so naturally, I overreacted and got upset every time he tried to share anything at all with me. We needed balance, and we needed to learn how to disagree agreeably.

Respect

Showing respect in our attitudes, voice tones, facial expressions and body language has been the key for us in learning how to disagree agreeably. Most people do not mind if you have a different opinion than they do as long as you don't make them feel as if their opinion is ridiculous and of no value. There is a wise way to talk to people and a way that is not wise.

Wisdom leads to peace and victory, but foolishness leads to disaster. I do not have to try to change another person's opinion. Much of what I used to call communication was manipulation. I was trying to manipulate the other person's opinion to agree with my own.

Dave could see my manipulation, and he started saying to me in those trying times, "Stop trying to convince me, Joyce. If I am wrong, let God convince me. If you are wrong, I will let God convince you." We both learned to say what we felt and thought, and if we disagreed, to drop it for a while and see what God did.

We learned to be respectful in the way we talked to one another. A facial expression can reveal our disrespect to another person. Voice tones or body language can do the same thing. If I let out a huge sigh when Dave is trying to share something with me, it is obvious to him that I do not consider what he is saying worth listening to. It says, "I have already made up my mind, and I am really not interested in hearing what you have to say."

You may notice that I keep saying, "I learned," "we learned," "I am learning" or "we are learning." It is important to understand that, first of all, being a peacemaker is a decision, and then it is a learning process. Don't be discouraged when you decide to abstain from strife, and then, occasionally, fall back into old ways. Just be determined to "learn." The Holy Spirit is your personal teacher. Each relationship is different, and the Holy Spirit will walk you through your unique situation as you trust Him.

I erected many walls in my life that I did not even know were there. Many of my reactions were based on old situations. Dave had nothing to do with the hurts from my past, but I had to learn how to react to him. The root of rejection had not been properly dealt with, and I often perceived rejection, when, in reality, that was not the case.

My perception was affected by years of abuse and control. I still had many issues that needed to be dealt with in order for me to enjoy total freedom. They obviously do not get dealt with all at one time. The Holy Spirit leads us as He sees best. We will cross the finish line in victory if we stick with the program.

Learning to disagree agreeably sometimes requires continuing to search for an answer both parties can be satisfied with. When Dave and I shop for household furniture, we often like two different things. Some men are not at all interested in helping to decorate their homes, but Dave has very definite opinions about what he likes. So do I. But our decorating tastes are very different.

Things that Dave thinks look well together and match nicely, often I think look terrible. Or, at times when I really like something, he doesn't like it at all. When we tried to shop for furniture, there was strife between us by the time we had been in the first store for twenty minutes. Shopping together was quite traumatic. By the time we got home, I was exhausted from the inner turmoil I had experienced during the trip.

Finally, we agreed to disagree agreeably. I realized that my opinion is no more right than his. Therefore, we agreed to continue shopping until we found something we both liked. Frequently, that required one or the other of us giving up the things we wanted and being willing to keep searching for something we could both enjoy. At times we gave up, went home and tried again another day.

As I look back at the difficulty we experienced making purchases, it amazes me. It is not that difficult now. What makes the difference? It's the way we learned to handle things. Differing opinions are not the problem—it's how we express the differing opinions that opens the door for strife.

Let God Do the Changing in Your Life

Our ministry is another area that challenged us. Dave often felt I was "running out ahead of God." I told him that his ministry was "waiting on God." Of course, I said it with sarcasm and disrespectful body language. Once I thought I had heard from God about something, I wanted to go for it! Dave wanted to wait a while and make sure it was God.

A couple of years ago Dave had a vision of what he and I were like back then. He saw me as a team of wild horses, and he held the reins, trying to hold me back and give me some direction. He was not trying to prevent me from fulfilling the calling on my life, but he did not want me to get in trouble.

We were both wrong. I moved too fast at times, and he moved too slow. That is exactly why we need each other. God often puts us with people who are not like us so we can serve as a balance for one another.

Sports were another problem. Dave loved all kinds of sports, and I did not enjoy any of them. His love for sports, and my lack of love for them, caused a great deal of disagreement in our household. Over the years we have learned to respect each other's differences, which has brought harmony and balance.

One day in the midst of a verbal disagreement, Dave looked at me and said, "Joyce, I am doing the best I know how to do."

"Well, so am I," I responded.

We were finally just plain tired of picking on each other all the time and bickering. We actually shook hands. "Dave," I said, "I want you to know that I accept you today just the way you are. I believe that you *are* doing the best you can."

"Joyce, I accept you today the way you are," Dave replied. "I believe you are doing the best you can, too."

That was a new beginning for us! We allowed each other freedom to be who we are. People need freedom to grow. But God can't change you if you stand in His way. God could not speak to Dave because I was too busy speaking to him. God could not change him because I was trying to change him. God needed my faith, not my works of the flesh. Set the people in your life free, and trust God to make whatever changes are necessary. This action will bring much peace into your life.

STEPS TO FOLLOW

There are several things that can help you disagree agreeably. We have discovered that respect is one of them. Another is understanding that love requires willingness to give up our right to be right. When we walk in love, we are not seeking what is best for ourselves, but what is best for the person we love.

It isn't easy to learn to walk in love because we are endowed with a generous portion of selfishness. That is part of the fleshly nature. If two people are willing to take turns giving in to the other, it will benefit the relationship. We don't have to keep a literal record of who got his way last, but it is good to keep in mind that no relationship is going to be healthy if any one party gets his way all the time.

Dave and I both "give in" regularly—in a balanced way. In other words, I don't get my way all the time, and neither does he. We both are willing to follow the promptings of the Holy Spirit as to who needs to back off this time.

There have been times when God would try to lead me to apologize to Dave when there was friction between us. But I would not do it if I had apologized to Dave last. I was willing to take my turn, but not willing to let go of legalism. I wanted to make sure I was not taken advantage of, and therefore, I kept mental lists of who got his way last.

Pride is another problem, and the only way to fight pride is with humility. Letting another do a thing his way when you heartily disagree requires humility. To be able to do so and keep a good attitude is a sign of maturity. If you give in and let someone else have his way, but spend the day feeling sorry for yourself, what advantage have you gained? None at all! You have simply closed one door in the devil's face and opened another one for him.

You will have to learn your own ways of disagreeing

agreeably, because as I have said, all situations are unique. All people are unique. If you are a believer in a relationship with an unbeliever, God may well require you to be the one who gives in more frequently simply because (hopefully) you have enough of the Word of God in your heart to enable you to do so. People who have no knowledge of the Word of God are led by feelings and thoughts. People grounded in the Word of God know that feelings and thoughts will lead to disaster.

With knowledge comes responsibility, so do not be surprised if the Holy Spirit places a level of responsibility on you that He does not seem to place on the spiritually immature partner. Your flesh may scream, "This is not fair!" But when I question God about something that seems unfair, He reminds me that Jesus' death on the cross was not fair—it was love.

Our love should measure up to God's love. We can learn to disagree agreeably. Our love may be tested in this area, especially in our relationships with our children.

LIFE WITHOUT STRIFE

STUDY QUESTIONS

CHAPTER 13
HOW TO DISAGREE AGREEABLY

God commands us not to get into strife. The Bible says, "The servant of the Lord must not strive" (2 Tim. 2:24, KJV).

1. How can you walk in bold determination to keep strife out of your life and relationships?____________________

2. How can you become a peacemaker without becoming a doormat?____________________

3. Have you ever refused to communicate your thoughts and feelings in an effort to keep peace? What was the end result?

4. Describe a situation in which strife was averted in one of your relationships. What kind of body language, facial expressions, voice tones and attitudes were displayed?__________

5. Now, think about a time when strife was not averted and tempers flared, feelings were hurt and division resulted. Describe the body language, facial expressions, voice tones and attitudes that caused the disagreement to escalate.

6. What peacemaking lessons can you learn from these situations?____________________

LIFE WITHOUT STRIFE

Study Questions

7. Describe a situation when you felt responsible for changing the opinions of another. What was the outcome? ______

______

8. Could you have respected that person's opinion without changing your own? ______

9. Suppose you were able to rewrite history. Describe the situation you just mentioned, only change the details to respect and honor the other individual's opinion, while still remaining true to your own feelings and opinions. ______

______

______

10. What strife-filled situations in your life are really minor differences of opinion when you look at the big picture? ______

______

______

11. How can you give others in your life the freedom to be who they are and show greater respect for their personal opinions and preferences? ______

______

______

12. Do you believe that God has the power and ability to make the necessary changes in your spouse and others in your life? Declare your trust in God's ability and intention to change others around you in ways that are necessary. ______

______

______

Dear Lord, I commit to allowing others the freedom to hold their own opinions and to make their own choices. I trust You to mold and shape others into the people You want them to be. Help me to learn new wisdom from You for relating to those around me. Help me to be a peacemaker in my attitudes, body language and facial expressions. In Jesus' name, amen.

Fourteen

Strife Between Parents and Children

Accepting people the way they are and trusting God to make the changes He sees fit applies not only to marriages, but to all relationships. Strife can creep into relationships between parents and children quickly.

Dave and I have four children. One of them has my personality; one has Dave's; and the other two have mixtures of our personalities and those of our parents.

People are born with various blendings of temperament. Personalities are formed over the years as a result of the natural temperament God has given us and the events that occur in the early, formative years of our lives.

You might think it would be easy to get along with someone who was just like you, but sometimes that is harder than adjusting to a totally different personality. The two of my four children with whom I had the greatest struggles were my oldest son (who has my temperament) and my oldest daughter.

She has developed discipline in her adult life, but growing up she had none.

David

Our oldest son, David, was so much like me that we continually had strife between us. Since we both have strong, "take charge" personalities, we were each trying to "take charge" of each other! I wanted him to do what I wanted him to do. He wanted to do what he wanted to do. And he wanted me to do what he wanted me to do.

Even as a toddler, he would insist that I sit and play with him. He did not want to play by himself at all. I always felt, in some vague way, that he was trying to control me. As he grew older, the problems only increased. I continually felt a struggle between us and really never understood what was going on.

I loved him, but to be very honest, I did not like him. I realized later that I did not like myself, so I naturally would not like him either since we were so much alike. Many parents have one child who is exactly like them, and they struggle with that child. We often see all the weaknesses we dislike about ourselves in one of our children. We must be careful to separate the weakness from the person. Otherwise, we may end up rejecting the person instead of trying to help him overcome the weakness.

I felt guilty because I did not like my son. I know that many of the people who read this book have experienced the same thing. Parents know they should love and accept their own child. When that seems to be impossible, guilt begins to accuse. Actually, I realize now that it was not even him that I did not like. What I disliked was being controlled. I loved him, but did not like the way he acted.

My abusive background had caused me to develop an out-of-balance sensitivity to strong personalities. Although a strong personality myself, I did not enjoy being around anyone else who was. I wanted to control—not be controlled.

If I could have understood what was happening between my son and me, at an early age I could have helped him learn to be strong in a positive way. Since I did not understand, I only increased the weaknesses in his temperament. He and I lived in continual strife, and it placed as much pressure on him as it did me.

Any child can sense when a parent is not happy with him. David knew down deep inside that I was not pleased with him, and he felt rejected. I was not giving him the liberty to be who he was, but, once again, as I did with so many people, I was trying to change him into what I would have liked him to be.

> Train up a child in the way he should go [and in keeping with his individual gift or bent], and when he is old he will not depart from it.
>
> —PROVERBS 22:6

I have learned a lot from the Amplified Bible translation of that verse. It does not say, "train up a child in the way you would like him to go." It states that we should train our children according to their own individual gifts or bents—according to the "spiritual markings" we see on our children.

Had I been more spiritually in tune, I would have recognized that God had built David for leadership and that He had given him the temperament to go with it. But instead of seeing that, all I saw at the time was that David made me uncomfortable, and I wanted him to change.

We had serious problems in our relationship for a long time. But the more I learned from God's Word, the more I realized I was not handling the situation correctly. I recall when God told me that I needed to forgive David for not meeting "my" expectations. He told me that I was in unforgiveness with my son because he was not what "I" wanted him to be. That realization was one big step toward healing in our relationship.

The Holy Spirit let me know that I needed to verbalize acceptance to David. I needed to let him know that even though I did not agree with all of his ways, I did love him and was willing to accept him where he was.

The healing process took some time, but from that point of forgiveness, we saw gradual change. David was about eighteen years old then. After a short period of time, God called him to go to Bible college. After college, he married and spent one year on the mission field in Costa Rica. When he and his wife returned from the mission field, he took a job with us. He is now a key leader in our ministry.

After he came to work for us, we had some serious struggles learning how to function together properly in all the different roles—parent and child; boss and employee; as well as Dave and I fulfilling the roles of spiritual leaders in his life.

He is still growing spiritually, but in God's plan. The very things that I struggled with so much in his personality as a child have become the biggest blessing to us in his role in the ministry. We need people with management gifts whom we can trust, and he is one of those people.

Laura

Our oldest daughter was my second great challenge as a parent. Laura was not an organized person—she forgot things, continually lost her belongings easily and got only poor-to-mediocre grades in school. If she remembered to do her homework at night, she might lose it before she got to school in the morning. Or if she took it to class and turned it in, she forgot to put her name on it and received no credit for having done the work.

She kept her room in shambles. When she came in the

door at night from school, she left a trail of personal belongings everywhere she went. Her coat was dropped in a chair, her keys thrown on the table, her purse dropped on the couch, her bookbag plopped on the floor in the kitchen and she herself would be in the middle of the bed talking on the phone!

I was born with organizational gifts and have always been a naturally disciplined person. I expected her to be the same. I talked and talked, trying to get her to understand. And when talking was not doing any good, I screamed and yelled.

After she graduated from high school, Laura came to work for Life In The Word. At that time, our offices were located in the lower level of our home.

Although we discussed with Laura the necessity of developing the employee/employer relationship, it quickly became apparent that her employment was going to present the opportunity for strife.

She was very young and had her own ideas about life and the way things should be done. She was already experiencing a mild case of rebellion. It was nothing serious, but she did not want anyone, especially Mom and Dad, telling her what to do.

There were mornings when she should have been downstairs working already, and I would discover her still in the bathroom combing her hair. Of course, I felt I needed to tell her she had to get to work on time. The fact that the office was in our home and that she was our daughter did not matter.

We tried to explain the principles of excellence to her. We reminded her that we had other employees to consider. She nodded in agreement, but each morning when I went down the steps to begin my work day, I could feel the strife coming up the steps to meet me. It was an "angry undercurrent," not open verbal disagreement. Outwardly, her response was, "OK, I'll do what you say." But in her heart she felt we were wrong.

There were times when she wanted to get off work early

to go somewhere with her boyfriend, and we had to say no. There were times when we felt she was spending too much time talking to him on the phone during working hours. I was more and more uncomfortable, and I became concerned that our relationship would be totally ruined if something was not done. I had tried to confront the problem, but it only seemed to make it worse. What should we do? Would we actually fire our own daughter?

God had instructed Dave and me that if we would keep strife out of our marriage and ministry, He would bless us. We were tested and tried in this area. We knew that the enemy was trying us. It was as if the devil was saying, "We'll see how serious you are about keeping strife out."

There are instances when a period of time away from someone will change the perspective about the entire relationship. Dave and I talked and prayed about it. We both felt that it would be better for our overall relationship with her if she worked somewhere else. We went to her, openly shared our feelings with her and she agreed.

Sometime later, she announced her plans to get married. More strife developed concerning our financial obligations for her wedding. Her relationship with me during the months before her wedding, and even on her wedding day, was rather cool. And even though she lived just fifteen minutes from our home, we rarely saw her or heard from her during the first six months she lived away from home.

One night as I lay crying in my bed, I turned to Dave and said, "Laura doesn't love me anymore." That was a very hurtful feeling for me, as it would be for any mother. When a child rejects his or her parents, the parents are tempted to feel like total failures in the department of parenting.

Dave tried to tell me that Laura would change her mind if I would give her some time. "She just needs some time on her own," he said. "She will find out that life is a little different than she thinks it's going to be. She will discover that Mom and Dad were not so bad after all."

Dave was right. After a while we started seeing her more often. We were very careful not to interfere in her business. We realized she was very sensitive about us telling her what to do. It would not be wise to even make suggestions to her. She quit going to church during those months and, of course, we were concerned. But we knew it was important not to hassle her about it.

We needed to love her right where she was and let God do what needed to be done. We prayed for her, loved her and waited. I am not saying we did it without emotional suffering. It was hard for us to see her stay away from church when we were in full-time ministry. God is number one in our lives, and we wanted her to make Him number one in her life.

After leaving her job at Life In The Word, she went to work at a law firm. She began to see some of the world and what it is really like. She went to church occasionally, but was not seriously committed to the Lord. She never stopped believing, but she was heading for trouble if she did not make a decision. As a Christian, you either go forward aggressively or you begin to backslide. You cannot be stagnant. If you're not pressing forward, you will go backward. As a parent, it is very difficult to watch your children struggle in this area, knowing that if you try to force spiritual growth on your children, you will only make matters worse.

Laura became unhappy after a period of time. She thought a new job would make things better. She went to work at a state school for the blind. She had always enjoyed helping people that were hurting, and she felt she would be happier there. It did help for a time because it was new. But soon, the same dissatisfaction returned.

We had told her when she left our ministry that the door would be open for her to return to work for us someday. But first she would need to make a spiritual commitment to God. By this time we had proven to her that we would accept her just the way she was. She knew we loved her. We could even talk with her about her need to get back to regular church attendance and stop drifting away from God. She agreed, but was not ready to work it out in her life.

Finally, the time came when she wanted to come back to work for us. She knew that she really needed to get committed all the way around. She knew how she would have to live her life in order to work for the ministry, and she believed coming back to work for us would help her follow through. We had some long talks, and we all agreed to give it another try.

Recently we celebrated her five-year anniversary at the ministry. All is well. She had a job in the office for quite some time, then the opportunity came for her husband to work for us as our soundman on the road. He held that position for quite a while before he was promoted to road manager.

He and Laura have done an excellent job. We get along very well, and everyone is happy. They, and their two children, are still on the road with us.

This began as one of those situations where being too close caused trouble. But we all matured and became wise enough to handle things. We were able to come back into good balance.

I am still amazed to realize how miserable I made myself trying to change people. It never worked. God has done with ease—and in a short period of time—what I was trying to do for years.

Parents must be careful not to break the spirit of the child. Harsh and undue chastisements can do just that. The child may be doing his best, and yet, if the parent is continually dissatisfied, it will weary the child and break his spirit. He will no longer want to try. He may give up and become rebellious as a means of defense against constant criticism.

> Fathers, do not irritate and provoke your children to anger [do not exasperate them to resentment], but rear them [tenderly] in the training and discipline and the counsel and admonition of the Lord.
>
> —EPHESIANS 6:4

Freedom is one of the greatest gifts we can give a person. Love liberates a person to be what God designed them to be. It does not try to manipulate them for personal gain. Love helps people overcome their weaknesses and eventually transforms them into the lovely creatures God had in mind initially. If you love someone, set him free, and if it's true love, he will come back to you.

My prayer is that by sharing examples from my personal life, you will be helped and prevented from making some of the mistakes I did. Or, if you are already experiencing the pain of a damaging relationship, you will make the decision to destroy strife instead of relationships. Perhaps you are ready to take a step of forgiveness.

CHAPTER 14
STRIFE BETWEEN PARENTS AND CHILDREN

The blending of temperaments, tastes and opinions within families can be a breeding ground for strife. Yet, none of us want to live a strife-filled home. Let's take a closer look at peacemaking within the family.

1. Describe the different types of personalities within your family. Are some family members passive? Are certain family members strong-willed? ______________________________

2. Do you have a child or children who are just like you?______

3. What personality clashes tend to create strife in your family?

4. What strategies has God given you for diffusing strife within your family?______________________________

5. What actions, attitudes or personality traits do you hold that tend to fuel family strife?______________________________

6. What principles from the Bible has God given you to minimize the strife that your personality traits cause in the family?

LIFE WITHOUT STRIFE

Study Questions

7. What weaknesses in family members do you find particularly annoying or difficult to deal with? ________________

____

____

8. How can you give these family members the freedom to grow without making them feel rejected? ________________

____

____

9. What weaknesses in yourself do you dislike? ____________

____

____

10. How can you give yourself freedom to be human? _________

____

____

11. Do you fall into regular ruts with certain family members, arguing, scolding or complaining about the same unresolved conflicts without experiencing any improvement?

____

____

12. How can you submit these ruts to the Lord and find more peaceful ways of dealing with these conflicts? ____________

____

____

Dear heavenly Father, I give You my family members, and I ask for Your peace in all of our interactions and conflicts. I thank You for creating each one of us with our weaknesses, annoying habits and different personality traits. Give us the grace to always see You in each other, to always love each other and to always love ourselves. In Jesus' name, amen.

Fifteen

Be Quick to Forgive

The faster we forgive, the less opportunity there is for strife to develop. When a person forgives freely, he also forgives quickly. Forgiveness closes the door to Satan's attack and refuses to give him a foothold that would eventually become a stronghold.

> Be gentle and forbearing with one another and, if one has a difference (a grievance or complaint) against another, readily pardoning each other; even as the Lord has [freely] forgiven you, so must you also [forgive].
>
> —Colossians 3:13

God's Word gives us many instructions about the dangers of unforgiveness, bitterness and resentment. Forgiveness can prevent or end strife.

Let's take a verse-by-verse look at a portion of Scripture in the eighteenth chapter of Matthew, where Christ is teaching His followers about forgiveness.

> Again I tell you, if two of you on earth agree (harmonize together, make a symphony together) about whatever [anything and everything] they may ask, it will come to pass and be done for them by My Father in heaven. For wherever two or three are gathered (drawn together as My followers) in (into) My name, there I AM in the midst of them.
>
> —Matthew 18:19-20

The Lord so desires harmony and unity that He promises to be right in the midst of any two or more people who will do whatever it takes to keep strife out of their lives and live in peace. He also tells us that this power of unity affects our prayers in a positive way. What peaceful people ask for they receive. Christ's presence in our lives alone is worth whatever we have to do to live in unity.

There is a direct correlation between peace and the presence of God. Desperately needing and wanting God's presence provoked me to do whatever was necessary to keep strife out of my life. We also have the additional promise of receiving answers to our prayers.

> Then Peter came up to Him and said, Lord, how many times may my brother sin against me and I forgive him and let it go? [As many as] up to seven times? Jesus answered him, I tell you, not up to seven times, but seventy times seven!
>
> —Matthew 18:21-22

I believe Peter was dealing with someone in his life who offended him regularly. They may or may not have been doing anything to provoke him. It may be that one of the other disciples was simply a continual thorn in Peter's flesh.

I can think of an individual in my life whom I have had to forgive numerous times in my life—and he doesn't even know he needs forgiveness. Forgiveness serves two purposes: It is available when a person who has offended you asks you to forgive him or her, and you do. But you also have the option of offering it to the person who did not intend to offend you and does not know he did, but you need to forgive him in order to keep yourself in peace.

At times people come up to ask me to forgive them for not liking me or for speaking unkindly about me. I wasn't aware of their problem. Their problem was not hurting *me*—it was hurting *them.* I gladly forgave them, because I wanted them to be free. On other occasions, someone may offend me without knowing it. I forgave them for my sake because I need to be released.

If Peter had not been facing a situation of continual offense, he probably would not have asked how many times he needed to forgive his brother. Peter thought perhaps he should forgive seven times, but Jesus told him to forgive seven times seventy. That represents whatever number of times it takes being willing to forgive to remain in peace.

> Therefore the kingdom of heaven is like a human king who wished to settle accounts with his attendants. When he began the accounting, one was brought to him who owed him ten thousand talents [probably about ten million dollars], and because he could not pay, his master ordered him to be sold, with his wife and his children and everything that he possessed, and payment to be made. So the attendant fell on his knees, begging him, Have patience with me and I will pay you everything. And his master's heart was moved with compassion, and he released him and forgave him [cancelling] the debt.
>
> —Matthew 18:23-27

This example represents a sinner who owes so much to God that he could never pay his debt. This man asks for forgiveness of the debt, and through the sacrifice of Jesus, all of his debts are cancelled. This occurred because of the mercy and compassion of our heavenly Father. "All have sinned and come short of the glory of God" (Rom. 3:23, KJV). Therefore, these verses represent all of us.

> But that same attendant, as he went out, found one of his fellow attendants who owed him a hundred denarii [about twenty dollars]; and he caught him by the throat and said, Pay what you owe! So his fellow attendant fell down and begged him earnestly, Give me time, and I will pay you all! But he was unwilling, and he went out and had him put in prison till he should pay the debt.
>
> —MATTHEW 18:28–30

The same man who was unable to pay his debt and asked for and received mercy was unwilling to give mercy to another in a similar situation. This is an example of our relationship with God and with other people. The Lord forgives our sins because He knows we could never pay Him what we owe, but we often refuse to release others from their offenses toward us.

> When his fellow attendants saw what had happened, they were greatly distressed, and they went and told everything that had taken place to their master. Then his master called him and said to him, You contemptible and wicked attendant! I forgave and cancelled all that [great] debt of yours because you begged me to. And should you not have had pity and mercy on your fellow attendant, as I had pity and mercy on you?
>
> And in wrath his master turned him over to the torturers (the jailers), till he should pay all that he owed. So

> also My heavenly Father will deal with every one of you if you do not freely forgive your brother from your heart his offenses.
>
> —Matthew 18:31-35

When we refuse to forgive other people, we open a door for the devil to torment us. We lose our freedom—the glorious freedom that God intended us to have as we follow His ways. God's love is free. He is also merciful, kind, forgiving and slow to anger. We often desire the freedom and blessings without wanting the lifestyle that goes with it. Forgiveness must become a lifestyle. As soon as someone offends you, respond with forgiveness.

Unforgiveness is a major problem in the world, but it is not limited to the world. Many Christians also have a stronghold in this area. The world we live in today is filled with hurt and hurting people, and my experience has been that hurting people hurt others.

Since there is much opportunity for offense, the willingness to forgive quickly is a great need. It would be wonderful if these problems were isolated to the world, and the church were immune to them, but we know this is not the case.

The devil works overtime among God's people to bring offense, strife and disharmony because he knows it will shut down God's power that is available to the believer.

Strife is dangerous. I encourage you to move beyond your feelings into the realm of decision. Love is not a feeling—it's a decision. Your decision to forgive can eventually provide a feeling.

Love is the only force that will override hatred, anger and unforgiveness. God is love, and we must walk in love to display His character. Love is an effort. It requires study and meditation on the Word of God concerning the love walk. In my case, it required extensive study—years of it.

At one time, I lived behind the walls I had built to protect myself from emotional pain. It took time for me to realize that I could not love as long as I lived behind those walls. As a matter of fact, I had to learn that I really could not love and be loved until I was willing to take a chance on being hurt. Love does hurt sometimes, but it also heals. I lived in strife because I was unwilling to give anyone who had hurt me a chance to do it a second time.

If someone offended me, I cataloged it in my memory banks and put up a wall to keep that person at a distance or completely out of my life. I held grudges against people, but in reality, the grudges were holding me. I was in prison.

The abuse in my life had ended, but the pain of it could never go away as long as I held it in my soul by refusing to trust God to vindicate me. He promises to bring justice if we will trust Him. It may require time, and the justice may come in a way we had not anticipated, but God will bring justice into the lives of hurting people who are willing to follow His plan. Learn to forgive those who hurt you! It is the first step toward recovery.

The Word of God teaches us that our faith will not produce positive results if we go to God with unforgiveness in our hearts.

> And Jesus, replying, said to them, Have faith in God [constantly]. Truly I tell you, whoever says to this mountain, Be lifted up and thrown into the sea! and does not doubt at all in his heart but believes that what he says will take place, it will be done for him.
>
> For this reason I am telling you, whatever you ask for in prayer, believe (trust and be confident) that it is granted to you, and you will [get it]. And whenever you stand praying, if you have anything against anyone, forgive him and let it drop (leave it, let it go), in order that your Father Who is in heaven may also forgive you your [own] failings and shortcomings and let them drop. But if you do not

> forgive, neither will your Father in heaven forgive your failings and shortcomings.
>
> —Mark 11:22–26

If you have not been able to forgive the person who hurt you seriously, it may be because you have allowed the enemy to deceive you into believing that you can't forgive them. Make this affirmation daily:

> I can and will forgive ________________ for hurting me. I can do it because God's Spirit is in me and enables me to forgive.

The church is filled with unbelieving believers. We call ourselves believers, but we don't believe we can do the things we know we should do. Take a more positive approach and be more aggressive against offense. Be quick to forgive! Freely forgive! Be generous in forgiveness! Remember how much God forgives you daily!

Be determined not to live in strife. Don't let strife steal from you the inheritance God has said is rightfully yours.

LIFE WITHOUT STRIFE

STUDY QUESTIONS

CHAPTER 15
BE QUICK TO FORGIVE

Forgiveness is the fire extinguisher that douses the flames of strife that might otherwise consume our lives and destroy our relationships. Learning to forgive quickly is a key to battling strife. Paul writes,"Be gentle and forbearing with one another and, if one has a difference (a grievance or complaint) against another, readily pardoning each other; even as the Lord has [freely] forgiven you, so must you also [forgive]" (Col. 3:13).

1. Describe a situation in your life in which strife was ended when forgiveness and pardon were offered and received.

 ____

 ____

2. Using Matthew 18:19–20 as a guide, describe the link that exists between unity and God's presence.______________

 ____

 ____

3. Write about an experience you've had in which the presence of God was lifted after strife entered.______________

 ____

 ____

 ____

4. At times we must forgive those who knowingly offend us and come to us seeking forgiveness. Are there other kinds of situations for which we should forgive? List some of them.

 ____

 ____

 ____

5. Who is hurt by your unforgiveness?______________

 ____

 ____

6. Matthew 18:23–30 tells us of an individual who could not offer forgiveness to another person, and therefore was placed into prison. What kind of present-day prisons are those who cannot forgive thrown into?

   ____

   ____

7. Have you ever experienced torment from the devil as a result of not forgiving someone? Describe the situation.

   ____

   ____

   ____

8. Have you prayed and felt that your prayer was not heard? Write a possible explanation based upon Mark 11:22–26.

   ____

   ____

9. God promises to bring justice and vindication into the lives of wounded individuals. Describe a situations for which you need God's justice and vindication. ____________

   ____

   ____

10. Can you give God your hurt or betrayal and choose to trust Him for His justice? Write out a prayer turning your situation over to God. ______________________________

   ____

   ____

   ____

Dear Lord, I thank You for being a God of justice and mercy. I trust You for Your justice in my life. I choose right now to let go of my need to seek justice for myself. I declare right now that I am choosing You as my Judge, and I will no longer stand in the place of my own judge. I forgive everyone who has offended me, including (speak out their names). I release them right now in the name of Jesus. In Jesus' name, I thank You for the freedom of forgiveness and repentance in my own life. Amen.

Sixteen

Strife Steals Our Inheritance

We are joint heirs with Jesus Christ. Jesus said in John 16:15, "Everything that the Father has is Mine. That is what I meant when I said that He [the Spirit] will take the things that are Mine and will reveal (declare, disclose, transmit) it to you."

Think about it. Everything the Father has is ours through Jesus. What does the Father have? He certainly does not have strife. Everything that He has ministers life to us. His kingdom is one of righteousness, peace and joy. Whatever is right standing with Him will produce right thoughts, words and actions. Supernatural peace and joy, not based on positive or negative circumstances, belong to the believer.

> Peace I leave with you; My [own] peace I now give and bequeath to you. Not as the world gives do I give to you. Do not let your hearts be troubled, neither let them be afraid. [Stop allowing yourselves to be agitated and

> disturbed; and do not permit yourselves to be fearful and intimidated and cowardly and unsettled].
>
> —John 14:27

In essence, Jesus was saying, "I am willing you My peace. I am going away, and the thing I desire to leave you is My peace." His special peace is a wonderful possession. How valuable is peace? What is it worth?

Peace was worth the shedding of Jesus' blood.

> But He was wounded for our transgressions, He was bruised for our guilt and iniquities; the chastisement [needful to obtain] peace and well-being for us was upon Him, and with the stripes [that wounded] Him we are healed and made whole.
>
> —Isaiah 53:5

The chastisement of our peace was upon Him. The punishment required and the payment due were placed on Him. He became the blood sacrifice that atoned for and completely removed our sin in order for us to live in peace. God's will for us is that we live in peace with Him, with ourselves and with our fellowman. He wants us to have peace in the midst of our current circumstances, peace in the morning, at night and all times in between. Peace is our inheritance!

Strife is the thief of peace. Even a minor degree of strife will steal some of the peace that is allotted for you. Peace and enjoyment of life go hand in hand. Satan comes to kill, steal and destroy, and he accomplishes his goal, at least in large measure, through strife. Jesus came that we might have and enjoy life. People can enjoy life more with an abundance of peace. Peace is glorious!

Peace of Mind

Peace of mind is a precious treasure. The devil steals peace of mind, our inheritance, by attacking us with worry, anxiety and confusion. Did it ever occur to you that confusion is strife in your mind? A person who is confused argues with himself. His thoughts fly back and forth in conflict with each other. A doubleminded man is not at peace. Yet, the Bible clearly teaches us that peace of mind is our heritage. It also teaches us how to obtain this peace of mind.

> Do not fret or have any anxiety about anything, but in every circumstance and in everything, by prayer and petition (definite requests), with thanksgiving, continue to make your wants known to God. And God's peace [shall be yours, that tranquil state of a soul assured of its salvation through Christ, and so fearing nothing from God and being content with its earthly lot of whatever sort that is, that peace] which transcends all understanding shall garrison and mount guard over your hearts and minds in Christ Jesus.
>
> —Philippians 4:6–7

> You will guard him and keep him in perfect and constant peace whose mind [both its inclination and its character] is stayed on You, because he commits himself to You, leans on You, and hopes confidently in You.
>
> —Isaiah 26:3

It is important to realize that peace is your inherited right. Otherwise, the devil may convince you that worry is your obligation when you have problems. Many mothers think they are not good mothers if they don't worry about their children. These Christian women love the Lord, but they haven't received a revelation on the dangers of strife.

Their minds are not peaceful; they are filled with worry, anxiety and turmoil. Upset emotions result. Worry leads to emotional upset. In John 14:27, Jesus advises, "Stop allowing yourselves to be agitated and disturbed."

Strife is not just a problem *between* people; it's often a problem *within* a person. What is going on inside of you? Is the atmosphere inside peaceful or strifeful?

> But no weapon that is formed against you shall prosper, and every tongue that shall rise against you in judgment you shall show to be in the wrong. This [peace, righteousness, security, triumph over opposition] is the heritage of the servants of the Lord.
>
> —Isaiah 54:17

Peace is our heritage. It is ours through the "blood line." The blood of Jesus brings it to me. It is mine! I am determined that the devil is not going to steal my inheritance through strife. Learn to recognize strife. Refuse to allow it in your life.

Allow God to reveal the root of your problem. Satan does not want you to know the real problem. He wants you to run around in circles, so to speak, always looking for something and never discovering anything. We do not war with flesh and blood. Many times our problems are not what we think, but have their roots in subtle, hidden strife.

In this way Satan deceives people. They spend their lives attempting to deal with the wrong issues. Start confronting the spirit of strife, and you will see many things begin to fall into place.

Keep strife out of your life; out of your thoughts, words and attitudes; out of your relationships. Be at peace with God, with yourself and with your fellowman. Peace belongs to you. Jesus has already given it to you. Begin to live in peace. Make a decision today: "I am finished with upset and turmoil; peace is mine, and I am going to enjoy it *now.*"

Heirs Share Suffering and Glory

Peace is glorious, but it would be unfair to you if I did not share with you that suffering is often the road to glory. Romans 8:17 brings this out clearly. "And if we are [His] children, then we are [His] heirs also: heirs of God and fellow heirs with Christ [sharing His inheritance with Him]; only we must share His suffering if we are to share His glory."

Jesus lives in glory at this very moment, but He had to walk the road of suffering to get there. He became obedient unto death. He died to His own natural desires and lived for His Father's will. Paul said, "I die daily" (1 Cor. 15:31). I believe he was saying, "There are a lot of things I would rather do, and things I would prefer not to do, but I say no and follow the spirit of God that is in me."

In order to live in peace and enjoy our inheritance, we need to choose to handle things properly in order to maintain peace on a regular basis. Being a peacemaker often requires suffering. It requires saying no to the flesh. That is suffering.

People can be deceived into thinking they must bear the burdens which Jesus already bore on the cross. The burdens of sin and suffering are lifted from us by the blood of Jesus. But there are certain sufferings we will be called upon to bear in order to live godly, holy, righteous, peaceful and joy-filled lives.

God has told us, "I set before you life and death; choose life" (Deut. 30:19, author's paraphrase). Making right choices can cause suffering when the flesh does not get its own way. I am sure you have discovered by now that your flesh has a mind of its own.

The flesh ministers death, but the Spirit ministers life. If we follow the flesh, death is the result. If we follow the Spirit, the reward is life. Choosing peace instead of strife will certainly reward you with life and all the blessings that it brings. But, initially, you may suffer in your fleshly parts in order to maintain this peace.

For example, I get up in the morning, and I am at peace. It is a lovely sunny day, and I have nice plans that will bring enjoyment to me all day long. If everything goes the way I planned, all will be well. However, things begin to happen that seem to indicate that *my* plan may not fully come to pass.

A phone call from the office informs me that our new phone system is not working properly, and a lot of our calls are not getting through. This information provides me with an opportunity to choose life or death. I can worry, or I can pray and cast my care upon Jesus. If I cast my care on Jesus, I will stay at peace. But my flesh pushes me to worry because it wants to take care of itself.

My fleshly mind wants to figure out why this trouble happened and what I can do to make sure it does not happen again. The devil uses this situation (which he has arranged to begin with), to provoke strife into my thoughts toward the company we purchased the phone from. If I am not careful, before long I will want to call and tell them what I think of them and their phone system.

Remember, when I got up in the morning everything was wonderful. If I let it, one phone call has the power to change my whole day and attitude. Making the right choice may cause me to suffer temporarily in some areas, but it will eventually produce glory in many others.

We often get out of balance in the area of suffering. Some believe we glorify God by our suffering. We say, "Let's just love suffering and never resist any trouble." Others believe the Christian should never suffer, never be uncomfortable and always get everything just the way he wants it.

We cannot live in the ditch on either side of the road of suffering. We need to steer our course straight down the middle of the road. We need balance—not extremes.

Suffering, in itself, does not glorify God. But maintaining a proper attitude during times of suffering and being willing to suffer in order to do His will does glorify Him. Right choices will bring glory into our lives.

I now live in glorious peace most of the time. I went through much suffering in order to come to this place. I had to learn to be quiet when I would rather keep talking. I had to learn to humble myself and apologize when I did not think I was wrong. As I made those right choices, my flesh suffered.

I had to be quiet when my husband thought he was right, when I would rather have argued and tried to prove that I had the answer. I had to walk away from conversations where people were being criticized and judged just to stay out of the strife I could sense. My flesh suffered because it was nosy and wanted to know everything.

Even something as simple as choosing to smile when you feel like screaming causes suffering in the flesh. Don't be afraid of "godly suffering." The right kind of suffering will produce glory. The apostle Paul wrote a letter to the Corinthians, saying something like this: "Even though my letter hurt you, I am not sorry that I wrote it because I know that later on it will produce good things in your life." (See 2 Corinthians 7:8.)

If you choose strife, you will suffer. Why not choose peace, which may provoke suffering in the flesh, but will also lead to victory? If you are suffering because of strife, it will only lead to more suffering and greater problems. Why not learn to suffer in a godly way, knowing it will lead to glory?

Satan is afraid of peace. If you can learn how to stay in peace, you will defeat him, and he knows it. Peace is actually spiritual warfare, as we will learn in the next chapter. Peace must be the umpire in your life. An umpire makes the decision that settles the matter. Each team may believe the call should be in its own favor, but it is the umpire who makes the final decision. And once he does, that ends the matter.

Let peace have the deciding vote in the choices you make.

If something cannot bring peace, cast it out. Don't live for the moment only. Use wisdom to make choices now that will satisfy you later on.

> And let the peace (soul harmony which comes) from Christ rule (act as umpire continually) in your hearts [deciding and settling with finality all questions that arise in your minds, in that peaceful state] to which as [members of Christ's] one body you were also called [to live]. And be thankful (appreciative), [giving praise to God always].
>
> —Colossians 3:15

When you are having a difficult time hearing from God, or being able to decide what you should do in a certain situation, follow after peace.

No one could write a book big enough to cover every circumstance that you will face. But the Holy Spirit has come to administer the heritage that Jesus died to give you. Peace is one of your inherited blessings. The Holy Spirit wants you to live in your inheritance, but the final choice is yours. Choose life! Choose peace! Choose to wage the warfare of peace.

LIFE WITHOUT STRIFE

STUDY QUESTIONS

CHAPTER 16
STRIFE STEALS OUR INHERITANCE

We are heirs of Christ, according to God's Word. Jesus said, "Everything that the Father has is Mine. That is what I meant when I said that He [the Spirit] will take the things that are Mine and will reveal (declare, disclose, transmit) it to you" (John 16:15).

But even though we have a rich, wonderful and powerful inheritance in Christ, far too few of us ever walk in what He has given to us. One of the reasons we do not is because strife robs us of our inheritance. Let's take a deeper look.

1. According to John 14:27, peace was a part of Jesus Christ's last will and testament to His people. If Jesus Christ spoke of peace right before He died, how important do you think peace is in His estimation? Why? ____________________

   ____

   ____

2. What was the cost of our peace to Jesus Christ according to Isaiah 53:5? ____________________

   ____

   ____

3. Read Philippians 4:6–7, and describe one biblical way of holding on to your peace. ____________________

   ____

   ____

4. According to Isaiah 26:3, what is another way to keep your mind in God's peace? ____________________

   ____

   ____

5. List some ways you have chosen suffering in order to kill the flesh and bring peace into a situation. ____________________

   ____

   ____

6. Write about a time when you blew it and gave your flesh the upper hand and peace was lost. ___

7. Explain how love could be used as a spiritual weapon to defeat the strategies of Satan in past, present or future relationship situations. ___

8. Using Ephesians 2:6 as a reference, explain how resting in Christ is a powerful key to maintaining peace in your life. ___

9. In Isaiah 41:10–16, God tells His people over and over again not to fear. How can you not fear if your emotions are telling you to be fearful? ___

10. Describe a time you chose to hold your peace, quit talking and even walked away in order to avoid strife. ___

Dear Lord, help me to walk in peace in all of my relationships. Show me more and more biblical strategies for maintaining peace. Holy Spirit, nudge me when strife attempts to enter into my heart and mind. Show me how to diffuse every situation with faith, love, confidence and joy. In Jesus' name, amen.

Seventeen

The Warfare of Peace

During the first several years as a charismatic Christian, I listened to a lot of teaching on spiritual warfare. I tried to learn all I could to defeat the devil because it was obvious he was giving me a lot of trouble. I wanted the upper hand for a change.

It seemed I gained no victory from applying all the methods I had learned. Then the Lord graciously shared some truths that have become a blessing in my life. He showed me that spiritual warfare "methods" are good—but they are only carriers, or containers, for His real power.

I was busy rebuking, resisting, casting out and off, binding and loosing, fasting and praying—and anything else that anyone told me to do. The results were minimal, and I was worn out. I was getting to the point of "spiritual burnout." This occurs when a Christian continues to do things that do not produce positive results.

God opened up a whole new way of looking at spiritual warfare when He challenged me to observe how Jesus dealt with the devil. As I did so, I did not see Him doing a lot of the things I had been doing. For example, I learned that remaining obedient is spiritual warfare.

Fight the Devil With Obedience

We often quote only a portion of James 4:7. I usually hear it quoted like this: "Resist the devil and he will flee." Therefore, I was busy resisting, but he was not fleeing. Then I saw the whole scripture: "So be subject to God. Resist the devil [stand firm against him], and he will flee from you."

The first part about submitting to God is equally as important as the second part about resisting the devil. I realized that I was not as concerned about *submitting* as I was about *resisting.* It was a relief to find that my obedience would cause the devil to flee from me.

The Ninety-first Psalm sheds new light on the ministry of angels in our lives.

> For He will give His angels [especial] charge over you to accompany and defend and preserve you in all your ways [of obedience and service].
>
> —Psalm 91:11

As we walk in obedience, angels assist us in our warfare. Angel assistance will surely make the task much easier. Angels do not just work in my behalf because I am alive, nor do they work in my behalf just because I believe Jesus is my Savior. They hearken to the Word of God. As we speak God's Word and walk in obedience and service to God and man, the angels move in our behalf and protect us from principalities and powers. This does not mean that we can never make a mistake or be unharmed. It does mean that we must be serious about a lifestyle of obedience.

The Holy Spirit also revealed that the love walk brings spiritual warfare. The devil cannot handle a lover! He could not control Jesus because He walked in obedience and love. Jesus was always loving people and being good to them. The Word of God instructs us to "keep ourselves in the love of God" (Jude 21).

This may have a deeper meaning than just staying in love. It may be saying you will keep yourself from much harm as you remain in love. The Scriptures tell us that in the last days "the love of the great body of people (the church) will grow cold" (Matt. 24:12). This verse tells us that "cold love" will be one of the signs of the last days. Yet, Peter admonishes us:

> Above all things have intense and unfailing love for one another, for love covers a multitude of sins [forgives and disregards the offenses of others].
>
> —1 PETER 4:8

The devil brings offense, disharmony and strife between people, but the antidote for the whole poisonous problem is love! We can rebuke all the devils in the world—literally scream at them until we have no voice left—but they will not flee from the person who cares nothing for obedience and the love walk.

Satan knows that Christians who "talk the talk" but do not "walk the walk" are powerless against him. His End-Time warfare strategy is to build a stronghold of cold love. In this way he can keep the church of Jesus Christ powerless, but by remaining in peace we can do spiritual warfare and defeat his tactics.

A PLACE OF HONOR

The believer is "seated in heavenly places with Christ Jesus." (See Ephesians 2:6.) *Seated* refers to rest. Rest and peace are equivalent to one another. The Book of Hebrews teaches us to enter the rest of God and cease from the weariness and pain of human labor. (See Hebrews 4:3, 10–11.) This rest is and has been available to us since Jesus came, died for us, was resurrected from the dead and ascended on high.

Rest is available, but we are encouraged to "enter" it. We enter the rest of God by believing His Word and by trusting in Him instead of ourselves or someone else. We actually do spiritual warfare while we rest.

> And do not [for a moment] be frightened or intimidated in anything by your opponents and adversaries, for such [constancy and fearlessness] will be a clear sign (proof and seal) to them of [their impending] destruction, but [a sure token and evidence] of your deliverance and salvation, and that from God.
>
> —Philippians 1:28

Constancy refers to being the same—stable and consistent. It is a sign to the enemy of his impending destruction. Our rest in peace and joy during the devil's attack literally defeats him. He cannot handle a believer who knows how to "hold his peace." Consistency is also an outward sign that we are trusting God. It is trust that moves Him to deliver us.

We benefit when we defeat the devil, but Jesus also benefits. It gives Him glory when we operate according to His Word. He is able to bless us with our inheritance in Him. Talking about the promises of God is encouraging, but possessing them is much better.

> Blessed (happy, fortunate, to be envied) is the man whom You discipline and instruct, O Lord, and teach out of Your law, that You may give him power to keep himself calm in the days of adversity, until the [inevitable] pit of corruption is dug for the wicked.
>
> —Psalm 94:12–13

God's plan is to work in our lives to bring us to the place when during times of adversity we can keep ourselves calm.

> Fear not [there is nothing to fear], for I am with you; do not look around you in terror and be dismayed, for I am your God. I will strengthen and harden you to difficulties, yes, I will help you; yes, I will hold you up and retain you with My [victorious] right hand of rightness and justice.
>
> Behold, all they who are enraged and inflamed against you shall be put to shame and confounded; they who strive against you shall be as nothing and shall perish. You shall seek those who contend with you but shall not find them; they who war against you shall be as nothing, as nothing at all.
>
> For I the Lord your God hold your right hand; I am the Lord, Who says to you, Fear not; I will help you!
>
> Fear not, you worm Jacob, you men of Israel! I will help you, says the Lord; your Redeemer is the Holy One of Israel. Behold, I will make you to be a new, sharp, threshing instrument which has teeth; you shall thresh the mountains and beat them small, and shall make the hills like chaff.
>
> You shall winnow them, and the wind shall carry them away, and the tempest or whirlwind shall scatter them. And you shall rejoice in the Lord, you shall glory in the Holy One of Israel.
>
> —ISAIAH 41:10–16

The following is my paraphrase of these verses:

> Don't be afraid of anything. Do not allow anything to get you upset. Don't start looking all around you at the circumstances; don't start worrying. Remain peaceful, I am your God. I will help you; I will hold you up. When we

> feel like we are going to cave in, we have His promise to hold us up!
>
> All those in strife against you, those who come at you with a spirit of contention and war, shall end up as nothing. So hold your peace. As you hold your peace, I can work because it shows that you are trusting Me.
>
> I am doing a new thing in you during these trying times. I am turning you into a new, sharp, threshing machine that will mow down the enemy. Your reward will be glory and joy.

Jesus defeated the enemy with meekness, gentleness, kindness and love. His followers wanted Him to set up an earthly kingdom and behave as an earthly king. They wanted Him to move against the enemy in the same way that they made war. But He taught them a different way to fight their battles: "But I tell you, Love your enemies and pray for those who persecute (hurt and abuse) you" (Matt. 5:44). He said:

> But I say to you who are listening now to Me: [in order to heed, make it a practice to] love your enemies, treat well (do good to, act nobly toward) those who detest you and pursue you with hatred, invoke blessings upon and pray for the happiness of those who curse you, implore God's blessing (favor) upon those who abuse you [who revile, reproach, disparage, and high-handedly misuse you].
>
> —Luke 6:27–28

This was a brand new way of thinking! Jesus had come to open up a "new and living way" (Heb. 10:20), one that would minister life instead of death.

Peace Will End the War

Seeing peace as spiritual warfare may be a new way of

thinking. It certainly was for me. I had spent all of my life trying to fight my own battles. I thought when I learned about spiritual warfare that my struggles would be over. After all, I had located the culprit behind my problems—taking authority over him would put an end to the misery.

Instead I ended up in a struggle with the devil that was not producing positive results, simply because I had the methods but not the power flowing through them. Peace, love and obedience are power! My mind says fight the devil with fury—not peace. But how can peace win a war?

Think about a natural war for a minute. What finally puts an end to it? One or both parties decide not to fight anymore. Even if only one party decides not to fight, the other one will eventually have to quit because there is no one to fight with.

My husband used to make me mad because he would not fight with me. I was upset and angry, and I wanted him to say just one thing so I could rail on and on. But when he saw that I was just looking for an argument, he would be quiet and tell me, "I am not going to fight with you."

Sometimes he would even get in the car and leave for a while, infuriating me even more. But the bottom line was I could not fight with someone who would not fight back. If we meet our battles with peace and respond to the upsets in life with peace, we will experience victory!

The methods that Jesus teaches us to use to be victorious are usually the opposite of what seems to make sense in our heads. He tells us to "give away what you have and you will end up with more than you started with" (Matt. 19:21). And, "The first shall be last, and the last shall be first" (Matt. 19:30). He teaches that "the way up is down, humble yourself and I will lift you up." (See Matthew 18:4; 23:12; James 4:6; 1 Peter 5:6.)

Jesus conquered with meekness. He ruled with kindness. He humbled Himself and was placed far above all other authority. If we can accept these principles even though our minds cannot comprehend them, surely we can also accept that peace is spiritual warfare.

When the Israelites found the Red Sea facing them and the Egyptian army chasing them, they became frightened and cried to Moses.

> Moses told the people, Fear not; stand still (firm, confident, undismayed) and see the salvation of the Lord which He will work for you today. For the Egyptians you have seen today you shall never see again. The Lord will fight for you, and you shall hold your peace and remain at rest.
>
> —Exodus 14:13–14

Notice that Moses told them to "hold their peace and remain at rest." Why? They were in warfare, and it was necessary for them to respond in peace in order to win the battle! God would fight for them if they would show their confidence in Him by being peaceful. When trouble comes, our first temptation is to get upset, speak out of emotions, start trying first one thing and then another and hope to find something that will work and turn the situation around.

All of these are unacceptable behaviors for the believer who is walking in faith. None of them will bring victory! You are instructed to "hold your peace." Jesus gave us peace. It is our inheritance. The devil regularly attempts to steal it, but it is ours, and we must hold on to it.

What God gives us is ours. But we can keep it, use it, lose it or give it away. Adam was given dominion, and he gave it to Satan, who is referred to as the god of this world. The Lord God did not create Satan to be the god of this world, so how did he obtain that title? Adam gave up what God had given him.

Let's not make the same mistake with those things that have been given back to us through Jesus Christ. Our inheritance is truly awesome. Peace is a portion of it—a very important portion.

Grasp the importance of peace. Let a holy determination rise up within you to keep your peace and enjoy it. Always remember to wear your shoes of peace when you go into battle. God supplies us with the armor of a heavily armed soldier. He equips us for battle with righteousness, truth, peace, salvation, the Word, faith and prayer. (See Ephesians 6.) Many of God's children carry their armor instead of wearing it. Don't carry your shoes of peace with you like a possession—wear them! They will lead you into the warfare of love.

LIFE WITHOUT STRIFE

STUDY QUESTIONS

CHAPTER 17
THE WARFARE OF PEACE

Spiritual warfare to defeat the devil can be accomplished through powerful weapons that we often hear little about—such as obedience, submission to God and peace. The Bible says, "So be subject to God. Resist the devil [stand firm against him], and he will flee from you" (James 4:7).

1. Why do you suppose submitting to God is just as important as resisting the devil? ________________________________

   ____

2. One of Satan's greatest strategies against Christians is to rob us of our love for one another. Using 1 Peter 4:8, describe how you can keep that from happening. ________________

   ____

3. Read Philippians 1:28, and describe what place rest has in defeating the enemy. ________________________________

   ____

4. Psalm 94:12-13 says:

   > Blessed (happy, fortunate, to be envied) is the man whom You discipline and instruct, O Lord, and teach out of Your law, that You may give him power to keep himself calm in the days of adversity, until the [inevitable] pit of corruption is dug for the wicked.

   Have you ever experienced peace and calm in the midst of a spiritual attack? Describe that time.

   ____

   ____

   ____

   ____

   ____

   ____

5. Paraphrase Isaiah 41:10–16, using your own words to describe God's promise to keep you at peace during life's storms. ______________________________

____

6. Have you ever experienced an attack from an individual to destroy your character, position or reputation? Use Matthew 5:44 and Luke 6:27–28 to describe how you might respond biblically. ______________________________

____

7. The principles of Christianity are often paradoxical. In other words, they seem completely upside down. Using the following scriptures, write about events from your own life that illustrate the use or lack of use of these principles.

- ❑ Matthew 18:4 ______________________________
- ❑ Matthew 19:21 ______________________________
- ❑ Matthew 19:30 ______________________________
- ❑ Matthew 23:12 ______________________________
- ❑ James 4:6 ______________________________
- ❑ 1 Peter 5:6 ______________________________

Dear Lord, give me the grace to respond to the battles in my life with obedience, peace and trust. I submit my life to You, knowing that You hold my future in Your hands. You can see all the battles I've gone through and the ones I will go through in the future. I submit my future battles to You before they even happen, and I ask You to cause me to triumph through the power of Your peace. Amen.

Eighteen

The Warfare of Love

One principle weaves a continuous thread throughout the Word of God: Evil is conquered with good. "Do not let yourself be overcome by evil, but overcome (master) evil with good" (Rom. 12:21). If we walk in love aggressively, evil will not be able to overtake us. Aggressive love is a decision—it looks for someone to bless. Love searches for opportunities to display itself. The power of love works in partnership with faith.

> For [if we are] in Christ Jesus, neither circumcision nor uncircumcision counts for anything, but only faith activated and energized and expressed and working through love.
>
> —Galatians 5:6

Faith is activated, energized and expressed through love. Many people consider themselves to be great people of faith, but if you watch the fruit of their lives, there is very little genuine love displayed. They may appear to be powerful, but true spiritual power is found in the facets and fruits of love.

> If I [can] speak in the tongues of men and [even] of angels, but have not love (that reasoning, intentional, spiritual devotion such as is inspired by God's love for and in us), I am only a noisy gong or a clanging cymbal.
>
> And if I have prophetic powers (the gift of interpreting the divine will and purpose), and understand all the secret truths and mysteries and possess all knowledge, and if I have [sufficient] faith so that I can remove mountains, but have not love (God's love in me) I am nothing (a useless nobody).
>
> Even if I dole out all that I have [to the poor in providing] food, and if I surrender my body to be burned or in order that I may glory, but have not love (God's love in me), I gain nothing.
>
> Love endures long and is patient and kind; love never is envious nor boils over with jealousy, is not boastful or vainglorious, does not display itself haughtily. It is not conceited (arrogant and inflated with pride); it is not rude (unmannerly) and does not act unbecomingly. Love (God's love in us) does not insist on its own rights or its own way, for it is not self-seeking; it is not touchy or fretful or resentful; it takes no account of the evil done to it [it pays no attention to a suffered wrong]. It does not rejoice at injustice and unrighteousness, but rejoices when right and truth prevail.
>
> Love bears up under anything and everything that comes, is ever ready to believe the best of every person, its hopes are fadeless under all circumstances, and it endures everything [without weakening]. Love never fails [never fades out or becomes obsolete or comes to an end].
>
> —1 Corinthians 13:1–8

The Facets of Love

Love is like a sparkling diamond; it has many facets. There are nine facets that we will look at.

- Patience
- Kindness
- Generosity
- Humility
- Courtesy
- Unselfishness
- Good temper
- Guilelessness
- Sincerity

How often does the absence of love open a door for the spirit of strife? Had love been there when strife knocked at the door, it would have found no entrance. Evil would have been overcome by good. Light overcomes darkness. Death is completely vanquished and swallowed up in life.

Here is a foundational truth upon which we base our faith: Jesus came to save mankind.

> How God anointed and consecrated Jesus of Nazareth with the [Holy] Spirit and with strength and ability and power; how He went about doing good and, in particular, curing all that were harassed and oppressed by [the power of] the devil, for God was with Him.
>
> —Acts 10:38

We respond to God's love that has been poured out through Jesus. His love draws us out of our old evil ways, and as we fellowship with Him, we are changed into His likeness. Our evil is swallowed up in His goodness.

Jesus went about "doing good" (Acts 10:38), and in so doing, He was protected from the devil. His love walk became the armor of light: "The night is far gone and the day is almost here. Let us then drop (fling away) the works and deeds of darkness and put on the [full] armor of light" (Rom. 13:12).

If we wear the armor of light daily, darkness will have to flee. Go into a dark room, turn on the light and watch how fast the darkness is swallowed up in the light! If you are battling the devil, you might do well to concentrate more on walking in love. I found in my own life that I was concentrating so much on defeating the enemy that I had no time to be good to anyone. My war with the enemy was making me sour instead of sweet.

Let's examine each facet of love and think about how it would keep strife out if it were in operation.

1. Patience

Strife comes into relationships because people display impatience with each other or with themselves. Strife is the opposite of peace and love.

2. Kindness

Being kind to a distraught person will act as a healing salve, but harshness only increases anger. Strife always lurks around looking for a crack to crawl through. "And the servant of the Lord must not strive; but be gentle unto all men" (2 Tim. 2:24, KJV). Kindness will keep strife out!

3. Generosity

"Love never is envious nor boils over with jealousy" (1 Cor. 13:4). Envy and jealousy are open doors for strife. When you are tempted with jealousy, respond with generosity and the evil will be swallowed up by the good.

I have had times when the spirit of jealousy attacked me relentlessly concerning someone else's ministry. I have discovered that the way to combat the enemy in this area is to turn the thing around on him. Instead of playing into his hands and resenting the person because of what they have, I frequently give to them so they can have more. I may not always "feel" like doing it, but I have found that it works. I don't desire to be jealous; I hate the feeling of jealousy and envy. It's an attack from the enemy, and I can overcome it with the facet of love called generosity.

4. Humility

Humility is the opposite of pride. We have already seen how pride is an open door for strife. Humble yourself and God will exalt you. It would be impossible to live without strife if there was no humility. Being a peacemaker requires humility. Pride goes before destruction (Prov. 16:18). Many relationships have been destroyed by a spirit of strife just because neither party would humble himself and wait for God to do the exalting.

5. Courtesy

Love is not rude and unmannerly. It is amazing how the words "please" or "thank you" can soften a command. Those who have authority and are in a position to tell others what to do could avoid a lot of rebellion by using better manners.

I am anointed for leadership and have always seen the ability to lead inherent in my temperament. I was "born a boss," but I try not to be bossy—there is a big difference. I am direct and straightforward. I am a "meat and potatoes" person. I eliminate the frills and just get to the main issue. This is a good quality, but it can also be abrasive if it is not tempered with courtesy.

We need the pleasantries of life. They may not be vital, but it's wise to use them. I am the boss, and I can simply tell people what to do. If they want to work for me, they will do it. But taking the extra time to be courteous causes people to want to work for us for a long time.

I encourage you to go the extra mile to be courteous with

your family and closest friends. I have found that we have a tendency to take liberties with those closest to us that we wouldn't consider taking with a total stranger. I recall the Holy Spirit correcting me years ago for the rude way I was speaking to my husband. He said, "Joyce, if you would be as courteous to your husband as you are to your pastor, your marriage would be a lot better." A lot of strife can be avoided by simple courtesy.

6. Unselfishness

The King James translation says love "seeketh not her own" (1 Cor. 13:5). "If anyone intends to come after Me, let him deny himself [forget, ignore, disown, and lose sight of himself and his own interests]" (Mark 8:34).

Jesus is love, and if we intend to follow His lifestyle, it will require the development of an unselfish nature. The seed for that nature is in us by virtue of Christ being in us, but it must be developed by choice. God has planted His seed in us, but we must water and care for it properly so it grows to the fruit-bearing stage. The giving up of oneself is no easy task. The flesh dies hard and fights relentlessly.

Strife was a constant visitor in our home when I was totally selfish. Over the years, as God has dealt with me, I have noticed that as selfishness goes, strife loses its nesting place. Selfishness is the breeding ground for strife.

7. Good temper

Love is not easily provoked; it is not touchy or easily angered (1 Cor. 13:5). Love is slow to anger (James 1:19). God is slow to anger according to the Word, and He is love. The development of the fruit of self-control is the answer to a quick temper.

We start by asking God to reveal the root of the problem. It may be rooted in various things. Past abuse of any kind can leave a person with repressed anger that needs to be dealt with. Pride is often the root of a quick temper.

My daughter had problems with anger and finally saw that it was rooted in perfectionism. I have learned that using self-control to control the emotion of anger is much easier than trying to deal with all the repercussions once I let lose my temper. I hate strife and its effects on people. A good temper will slam the door in strife's face.

8. Guilelessness

Love "thinketh no evil" (1 Cor. 13:5, KJV). Wrong, evil thoughts open the door for strife. We must be accountable for our thoughts. They will produce good or evil in our lives. Each man has both the mind of the flesh and the mind of the spirit. (See Romans 8:6.)

We are to choose the mind of the Spirit. It produces life and peace. Love is good and expects the best of every person.

How is it possible to expect the best from people who have disappointed us time after time? Love forgets the past and deals with each issue in a fresh way. Oh, how glorious it would be to be totally guileless. Just imagine the inner peace in the person who never had an evil thought. You may think, ***This sounds great in theory, but is it really possible?*** I do not know if I will ever attain this perfection, but I am determined to press on toward the goal. Lovely thinking defeats strife!

9. Sincerity

Love is sincere. It's not just a lot of talk or theory but is seen in action. Love meets needs. Love is genuine. It really wants to help others. "[Let your] love be sincere (a real thing); hate what is evil [loathe all ungodliness, turn in horror from wickedness], but hold fast to that which is good" (Rom. 12:9).

This is the attitude we should have toward strife—we hate it because it is evil! It comes like a raging storm and leaves destruction everywhere it is permitted to go. Defeat it by holding fast to that which is good.

Love is the greatest thing in the world. It makes life worth living. Love sets us free from the Law. "And so faith, hope, love abide . . . but the greatest of these is love" (1 Cor. 13:13). Paul instructs us that love is "the more excellent way" to live (1 Cor. 12:31.) He prayed that "your love abound . . . and display itself" (Phil. 1:9).

Abounding love can overcome strife. Love will protect you from the devil. It is truly spiritual warfare. Satan knows this, so he fights those walking in love. He knows that if you develop your love walk, you will be dangerous to the kingdom of darkness.

I have studied love for many years, and it must remain a part of my regular study of God's Word. It is quite easy, because of the nature of the flesh, to become selfish and self-centered. But with God's help and a willing heart, we can meet strife and all that it represents with a true spirit of love and see it defeated every time.

LIFE WITHOUT STRIFE

Study Questions

Chapter 18
The Warfare of Love

The Bible teaches that good triumphs over evil: "Do not let yourself be overcome by evil but overcome (master) evil with good" (Rom. 12:21). By aggressively pursuing love, evil will not be able to overtake us.

1. Paraphrase 1 Corinthians 13:1–8 using your own words.

2. Think about a time in which you or another person was embroiled in strife. How could love have produced a different outcome? Explain.

3. How is love an armor of light according to Romans 13:12?

4. Generosity overcomes jealousy. Using 1 Corinthians 13:4, describe how jealousy can be defeated in your own heart through generosity.

5. Think about a situation you were in that was filled with strife. How could unselfishness have prevented that strife from occurring?____

6. Do you tend to think the worst of people and let them prove themselves otherwise? Apply 1 Corinthians 13:5 to these situations in your life.____________________________

Lord, teach me to win the battle against strife in my life through the power of Your love. Help me to walk in unselfishness, generosity and good will toward others. Where my heart is small, make it large with Your love. Where my love has failed, fill up the balance with Your own. Lord, give me a gift of love toward others, and teach me to walk in the ways and wisdom of Your divine love. Amen.

Nineteen

How Strife Affects the Anointing

The anointing of the Holy Spirit is one of the most important things in my life and ministry. His anointing ushers me into the presence and the power of God. The anointing manifests in ability, enablement and strength. The anointing ministers life to me. I feel alive and strong physically when the anointing is flowing. I am mentally alert when the anointing of God is manifesting.

God's anointing is always resident in the believer.

> But you have been anointed by [you hold a sacred appointment from, you have been given an unction from] the Holy One, and you all know [the Truth] or you know all things. . . .
>
> But as for you, the anointing (the sacred appointment, the unction) which you received from Him abides [permanently] in you; [so] then you have no need that anyone should instruct you. But just as His anointing

> teaches you concerning everything and is true and is no falsehood, so you must abide in (live in, never depart from) Him [being rooted in Him, knit to Him], just as [His anointing] has taught you [to do].
>
> —1 John 2:20, 27

The anointing is always in us, but the manifestation of the anointing is vital to powerful living and powerful ministry. Strife will definitely hinder the flow of God's anointing. The Holy Spirit gives the anointing, and strife grieves Him.

> And do not grieve the Holy Spirit of God [do not offend or vex or sadden Him], by Whom you were sealed (marked, branded as God's own, secured) for the day of redemption (of final deliverance through Christ from evil and the consequences of sin).
>
> Let all bitterness and indignation and wrath (passion, rage, bad temper) and resentment (anger, animosity) and quarreling (brawling, clamor, contention) and slander (evil-speaking, abusive or blasphemous language) be banished from you, with all malice (spite, ill will, or baseness of any kind).
>
> And become useful and helpful and kind to one another, tenderhearted (compassionate, understanding, loving-hearted), forgiving one another [readily and freely], as God in Christ forgave you.
>
> —Ephesians 4:30-32

Strife grieves the Holy Spirit. It will separate us from the power and anointing of the Spirit, but the power of peace binds us to the Holy Spirit.

> Be eager and strive earnestly to guard and keep the harmony and oneness of [and produced by] the Spirit in the binding power of peace.
>
> —Ephesians 4:3

One might say that peace and power live together. They are married; they support each other. Psalm 133 tells us that the anointing and unity are synonymous.

> Behold, how good and how pleasant it is for brethren to dwell together in unity! It is like the precious ointment poured on the head, that ran down on the beard, even the beard of Aaron [the first high priest], that came down upon the collar and skirts of his garments [consecrating the whole body].
>
> —Psalm 133:1–2

When kings and priests were anointed for their offices under the Old Covenant, oil (representing the Holy Spirit) was poured upon their heads and allowed to run down their beards upon the collar and skirts of their garments. Unity has the same effect. If unity produces the same results as the anointing, then strife—the opposite of unity—would produce the opposite results.

Strife blocks the flow of the anointing. It is no wonder that Jesus and the apostles taught the importance of forgiveness. Jesus declared that He was anointed by God to preach the good news and to bring healing to man physically, emotionally and spiritually. (See Isaiah 61:1–3; Luke 4:18). Jesus was referred to as the Prince of Peace. (See Isaiah 9:6.) As the anointed Prince of Peace, Jesus is a model to show us how the anointing and peace work together.

In the tenth chapter of Luke, Jesus sent seventy men out into the neighboring towns where He was going to visit. He told them to heal the sick and tell the people that the kingdom of God had come close to them. He instructed them to find a house and say, "Peace be to this household!" If peace settled there and remained, they could remain. If not, they were to move on to another town.

> Now after this the Lord chose and appointed seventy others and sent them out ahead of Him, two by two, into every town and place where He Himself was about to come (visit). And He said to them, The harvest indeed is abundant [there is much ripe grain], but the farmhands are few. Pray therefore the Lord of the harvest to send out laborers into His harvest. Go your way; behold, I send you out like lambs into the midst of wolves.
>
> Carry no purse, no provisions bag, no [change of] sandals; refrain from [retarding your journey by] saluting and wishing anyone well along the way. Whatever house you enter, first say, Peace be to this household! [Freedom from all the distresses that result from sin be with this family].
>
> And if anyone [worthy] of peace and blessedness is there, the peace and blessedness you wish shall come upon him; but if not, it shall come back to you. And stay on in the same house, eating and drinking what they provide, for the laborer is worthy of his wages. Do not keep moving from house to house.
>
> —Luke 10:1–7

Several years ago I felt led to teach on the subject of peace. I spent an entire day sitting in the middle of my bed studying. I felt as if I were looking for something concerning the subject of peace, and yet I did not know what it was. I searched the Scriptures, waiting for the light of revelation to come to me.

Finally, I saw something in these verses in Luke 10 that I had never seen previously. I felt the Lord was showing me that peace and power go together. The disciples were sent out to heal the sick and proclaim the kingdom of God. One of their instructions was to find a peaceful place to reside and stay there. I felt the Holy Spirit saying to me, "Joyce, if you want to have a powerful ministry that will helps multitudes, find peace and stay in it."

At that time I was not very peaceful. I still had a lot of

inner turmoil, and I still caused a lot of upset. I had not yet learned the importance of strife-free living. The Spirit showed me that just as He told the disciples to find a peaceful place and let that be their base of operation, I was to be His house—His base of operation—and He wanted the house He was working in to be peaceful.

I wanted to minister under a strong anointing, and I prayed about it regularly. God was answering my prayer by showing me what I needed to do to enable the anointing to flow.

The believer has God's anointing within. The person called by God to a ministry has the anointing resident in him to do what God has called him to. But sometimes there are things in the believer's life that must be moved out of the way in order to allow the anointing to flow.

I began to notice how the devil would often attempt to stir up strife between Dave and me just before a seminar where we would be ministering. I started to see a pattern.

I also realized why our family had experienced such strong attacks from Satan on Sunday mornings for so many years. The Bible teaches us that the seed of God's Word must be sown in a heart of peace by someone who works for and makes peace.

> And the harvest of righteousness (of conformity to God's will in thought and deed) is [the fruit of the seed] sown in peace by those who work for and make peace [in themselves and in others, that peace which means concord, agreement, and harmony between individuals, with undisturbedness, in a peaceful mind free from fears and agitating passions and moral conflicts].
>
> —James 3:18

Careful examination of this Scripture sheds light on the reason the devil attempts to upset people just before they are going to hear the Word of God and have an opportunity to advance in their walk with Him. The enemy also comes immediately after the seed is sown, hoping to steal the Word.

> The sower sows the Word. The ones along the path are those who have the Word sown [in their hearts], but when they hear, Satan comes at once and [by force] takes away the message which is sown in them.
>
> —Mark 4:14-15

Satan is intent on stealing the Word before it takes root in you. He knows if it takes root in your heart that it will begin to produce good fruit. We must operate in the wisdom of God from within and show ourselves wiser than the enemy. We cannot sit by passively and allow him to get us so upset before we get to church that we cannot hear or retain what is being said. Nor can we allow him to get us upset after we leave.

It's important for us to be able to think about the Word that has been preached and taught to us.

> And He said to them, Be careful what you are hearing. The measure [of thought and study] you give [to the truth you hear] will be the measure [of virtue and knowledge] that comes back to you—and more [besides] will be given to you who hear.
>
> —Mark 4:24

Satan will often attack your mind after hearing the Word lest you begin to meditate on it. I can remember our family arguing all the way to church on Sunday mornings, but living in pretense that all was well as soon as we saw anyone we knew. I would "fake" my way through the service, clapping at all the right places, saying "Amen!" at the appropriate times and pretend to pay attention to the pastor while he preached.

All the while, I was planning how I would ignore Dave or the kids until they apologized to me. I certainly did not intend to go home and fix them a nice dinner. I really did not even plan to talk to them. Satan delighted in those "flesh" days.

I was deceived. I did not understand what was going on. Everything would be fine one minute, and the next thing I knew, everyone would be mad—screaming and yelling. Or, to the other extreme, everyone would be deathly quiet—so cold and quiet that it was obvious feelings were hurt and wrong thoughts were running rampant. Strife is bickering, arguing, heated disagreement and an angry undercurrent. We definitely had strife, and I believe a lot of other families and individuals do also.

Is Satan deceiving you as he did me? Do you find that he works overtime trying to upset you before or after you have heard the Word or read the Word? He would rather keep you home, but if you're going to go, at least he wants you to go upset so you get nothing out of the service.

Beware of his deceits and strategies. Resist him at the onset. Do not give him time to work in your life. He is going to try to kill, steal and destroy you. Refuse to put up with it.

No matter how anointed a speaker is, that anointing will not have any effect on you if you're in strife when you get there. The anointing and strife do not work together, but the anointing and peace do. It is important that both the speaker and the listeners are peaceful. The seed must be sown in peace by someone who works for and makes peace (in themselves and in others). As a minister, this means that I must stay in peace myself and be a peacemaker if I desire a strong anointing flowing forth from me to help people.

As we travel and minister in various churches, I have found it interesting to note how often pastors come to church in separate cars from the rest of their families. At first, I thought this was a bit unusual, but some of them shared a twofold reason for doing so. First, many pastors like to get to the church early to pray and meditate on their sermon. And second, they want to be peaceful when they get there, and they have found that it is easier to stay peaceful if they drive by themselves.

Choose to Be a Peacemaker

Even normal noise can be upsetting to a person who has a lot on his mind. Just before one of our services, I am busy meditating on what God has given me to minister that day. I do not hide from my family, but I have asked them to refrain from telling me anything right before a meeting that would tend to be upsetting. They help me by trying to keep the atmosphere peaceful. You can also help your loved ones by maintaining peace, especially when you know they are already under pressure.

When a husband comes home from an especially trying day at the office, his wife can minister peace to him by directing the children into an activity that creates a calmer atmosphere, rather than a chaotic one.

When the wife has been cleaning and cooking all day for a special holiday family get-together the next day, the husband can minister peace to her by taking the children somewhere for the evening and allowing her to have a nice long block of quiet time.

If a child has been taking final exams for a week and is already under stress, the parents might choose to withhold correction for his messy room or leaving his bike out on the driveway until the stress of the exams has ended.

We can help each other to avoid strife by being a little more sensitive to one another's needs. Sow good seeds, and you will reap a good harvest in your own time of need. After being married to Dave for more than twenty-nine years, I can tell when he is tired or not feeling good. I have learned to minister peace to him at those times, instead of bringing up a problem to him right then.

He is a very peaceful man and would probably handle

himself quite well even if I did bring up a problem, but there is no point in adding weight to an already heavy load. The devil likes to place heavy loads on us that are hard to bear and then keeps pressing until we blow. But the Word of God teaches us to watch out for one another. This is part of the love walk.

> Strive to live in peace with everybody and pursue that consecration and holiness without which no one will [ever] see the Lord. Exercise foresight and be on the watch to look [after one another], to see that no one falls back from and fails to secure God's grace.
>
> —Hebrews 12:14–15

Grace is unmerited favor. We can simply do someone a favor and help him by not placing undue pressure upon him during tedious times. For me, it is when I am getting ready to minister. Satan is looking for any crack to crawl through. For you it may be some other area, but we all have them. He seeks to get us in strife so the anointing cannot flow.

There is an anointing for everything that we are called to do—not just for spiritual things. People laugh when I say this, but there is an anointing that comes on me to shop. If it's there, the trip is very fruitful and enjoyable. If it's not, I cannot find anything I am looking for. I can't seem to make decisions about what to buy. Even if I find something I like, I don't seem to have any real desire to buy it. I say in times like that, "If I buy anything today, it will have to jump off the rack and just get on my body."

One evening recently, Dave and I went shopping. We stopped to get a sandwich and were intending to spend the evening together at the mall. I needed to get a birthday present for our daughter and just wanted to look around. Dave usually enjoys that, but this particular evening he became extremely tired about thirty minutes after we got there.

I was just getting into my shopping, when he started rushing and hurrying me to get something so we could go. I felt hurt and offended. I could feel the strife come in immediately and the anointing disappear. All of a sudden, I wanted to leave. I was not feeling peaceful.

I had been working hard and had not spent as much personal time with Dave as I like to. I was really looking forward to having the evening with him, and when he acted as if he did not want to be there, I immediately had to start fighting anger, unforgiveness, strife, negative thoughts and tears.

I knew it was an attack, but that did not make it any less real. Dave knew I was having a hard time controlling my emotions, so he stayed very quiet. We left the parking lot and started home. We had just gotten on the highway when we came within an inch of having a car accident. If we had not been spared by what I believe were God's angels, we would have been hit on both sides at once.

What started out to be a lovely evening had suddenly turned into a chaotic mess of upset and strife. This is just the way the spirit of strife operates. They try to catch you off guard, or at a time when you're tired and more likely to give in rather than resist them.

Dave told me later that it was unbelievable how bad he felt and how fast it came on him. He had been fine when we got there, and suddenly he felt he could not stand to stay.

You might think it sounds a bit out of balance to talk of being anointed for such things as shopping, cleaning house or other ordinary chores. However, I firmly believe that God's Spirit is available to help us do anything that is the Lord's will and that's in His timing.

I do not think we should struggle with anything, and I believe we should enjoy everything. It's hard to truly enjoy anything without the anointing. God's presence makes everything easy and enjoyable. I believe a woman can go to the grocery store and be anointed by God to shop for her family's groceries if she will exercise her faith to release the anointing. If she gets upset with the grocery store because they don't have some items she wants, the anointing will stop flowing for her trip until she returns to a peaceful state and the strife disappears.

Strife can, and often does, affect us first in our attitude. One day I overheard a woman railing on and on about the postal system and the post office. After listening to her about late mail deliveries, lost packages and the cost of postage, I thought, *This woman is in a full-blown state of strife with the postal system.* As long as the strife was in her heart, she certainly could never enjoy going to the post office. Even talking about it upset her.

I was in strife with a dress shop once. I had purchased a dress there which fell apart. The store refused to take it back. I got very upset about it and told everybody I talked to about this dress shop and their poor customer service. I enthusiastically discouraged anyone who would listen from going there to shop. Whenever I passed this shop while walking in the shopping mall, I began to feel upset. If anyone was with me, I would repeat the story and get even more upset.

I did not have the revelation then that I do now on strife. God began to show me that I needed to forgive that dress shop for its policies that did not leave room to meet my need. It was a new level of learning for me regarding forgiveness. I knew about forgiving people, but not places. I learned that being in strife with a place is just as dangerous as being in strife with a person. The only difference is a place has no feelings, but it still affects the person in strife the same way.

What other kinds of things may we expect to be anointed for? I believe there is an anointed sleep we can enjoy when we go to bed at night. However, if a person lays in bed and thinks of some strifeful situation, he is not likely to enjoy his night's sleep. He may dream fretful dreams or toss and turn all night.

I believe there is an anointing to go to your workplace and enjoy being there. The anointing will also help you do your job with ease. Again, if you have strife with your boss or with other employees, the anointing will be blocked. Whether this is open strife or hidden within your heart, the effect is the same.

There is another revelation in the second verse of Psalm 133. When the priests were anointed, the oil was first poured on their head. Then it ran down on the collar and skirt of their garment. God called my attention to this principle: *The anointing flows down from the head.*

My husband is anointed to lead our family. If I am in strife with him, the anointing that is upon him will not flow down to me, and I will begin to sense struggle in our relationship. It can affect other family matters that could be handled with ease if I stay under his covering.

There is an anointing that rests on the head or the leader of a company, even if you don't like him or agree with him. When an individual is in strife with the head (open or underlying), the anointing cannot flow down to that person, and his job will be a struggle. He will dread going to work. He may even make foolish mistakes. Although he knows he is qualified to do the work, for some reason he keeps making errors.

This is a life principle. God has designed leadership to preserve order. God called Moses and anointed Aaron to help him. When the job became too much for them, God allowed Moses to anoint others to head up smaller groups of people. Each group had a captain, and even the captains had a leader. It's God's way, even if we don't like it.

Rebellion

Rebellion and strife go together. Where there is strife, there will also be rebellion, confusion and every evil work. (See James 3:16.) There is safety in leadership on a natural level.

If an employee does what the boss tells him, the employee is relieved of responsibility for the decision.

A godly response to those in authority over us also provides spiritual safety for us. If I will submit to authority for the sake of honoring God and His Word, I will enjoy a free flow of His anointing in my life. If I rebel and refuse to submit, I will block the anointing. I believe submission protects me from demonic attack, whereas rebellion opens the door for it.

Protect the anointing on your life by keeping the strife out. Live by the anointing. God has given it to you to help you in all that you do. Things are not accomplished by might nor power, but by His Spirit. (See Zechariah 4:6.) Stay peaceful and calm; be quick to forgive, slow to anger, patient and kind.

Can you imagine Jesus ever allowing the devil to push Him to lose control of His emotions? Jesus operated in perfect self-control. He did it for the sake of the kingdom and in order to complete the work He was sent to do. He declared that He was anointed to do certain things, and it is evident by studying His life that He was not going to permit a spirit of strife to hinder His mission.

Jesus had multiple opportunities to be in strife, and yet, without hesitation, He turned every one of them down. Even as He hung on the cross He prayed, "Father, forgive them for they know not what they do" (Luke 23:34). Judas, Herod, Pilate and the Pharisees all presented Him with opportunities for strife. He turned every one of them into an opportunity to show forth His Father's character. Instead of strife, He responded with gentleness, courtesy and patience.

I encourage you to meet the devil head on! Don't give up the anointing upon your life in order to satisfy some fleshly emotion that is pushing you to act like the devil instead of God.

CHAPTER 19

HOW STRIFE AFFECTS THE ANOINTING

The anointing of the Holy Spirit is resident in you to empower, strengthen, enlighten and equip you for ministry.

1. Strife and bitterness grieve the Holy Spirit. According to Ephesians 4:30–32, what is the scriptural antidote for strife? ____________________

2. In the same way that strife repels the Holy Spirit, the power of peace binds the Holy Spirit to us. What attitudes will help you to never grieve the Holy Spirit, according to Ephesians 4:3? ____________________

3. The Lord sent the disciples to go out and find a "base of operations" that was peaceful. Read Luke 10:1–7 and explain why you believe the Lord gave this command. ____________________

4. Is your "base of operations" peaceful, whether that be your home, your job, your church or your circle of friends? ____________________

5. What can you do to make your environment more peaceful? ____________________

6. Have you ever gotten into strife just before hearing the Word of God? Describe the time or times that it has happened. ____________________

7. What do you suppose was Satan's agenda in creating strife?

8. What strategies can you employ in the future to keep this from happening again?

9. How can you administer peace to an individual whose life often becomes embroiled in strife?

10. Have you ever felt offended by a bank, store or organization? What should you do to keep your heart free from strife in this matter?

11. Are there any situations in your life in which rebellion, either your own or someone else's, has opened a door to strife in your environment?

Dear Father, grant me the grace to live in and operate in an environment of peace. Show me what attitudes and habits I have that might be contributing to strife. Provide me with Your divine strategy for being a peacemaker wherever I go. In Jesus' name, amen.

Twenty

The Stress of Change

During times of change, strife has the opportunity to enter in. Not everyone likes change. Even if the change is positive there will be those that may be unhappy about it. For example, an employer may feel that he needs to make changes, but all the employees won't necessarily agree.

We've had to make certain changes as our ministry grows. Things we could do in the early days when we had five employees just won't work now. We changed our working hours recently and extended lunch hours. We had previously established our work day as 8:00 A.M. to 4:30 P.M., allowing thirty minutes for lunch. When we went on television with our ministry, we wanted to keep the office open as long as possible for people to place orders for tapes. None of our employees complained, but I am sure that some of them liked the change while others did not.

We all have personal preferences for things. Some changes

work out better for us than others. That is why people who are in charge of an organization must do what will be best for the overall operation and not just try to please all of the people. Nobody can please everybody all the time simply because people are very different.

We have noticed that when a pastor feels the Holy Spirit is leading him in a new direction, some of the congregation will agree and others will not. Much of the way people feel is based on personal preference, but it's a mistake for a person to assume that his leader is not following God's will just because he doesn't agree personally with the change.

For example, a pastor may feel that God is leading the church into a strong foreign missions outreach program. Some of his congregation may think it's great, while others may feel that an inner-city outreach program would be better. When people fail to realize that many of their feelings are based on their own opinions and preferences, they can quickly open a door for strife by vocalizing their disagreement.

An unbelievable amount of strife is stirred up in churches and brings destruction due to changes that not everyone understands and agrees with. I tell people who come to us with their problems that they should first give the changes a little time and see where they settle. Then they should talk to the pastor about their concerns, not to other members of the congregation. Often a little understanding of the situation can change your entire outlook on something.

Finally, if you find that you cannot be happy at the church any longer because of the changes, find another place to go—but leave in peace. Do not leave assuming that everyone else is wrong. What they are doing may be right for them but not right for you. We are to give one another liberty and not be judgmental.

> One [man's faith permits him to] believe he may eat anything, while a weaker one [limits his] eating to

> vegetables. Let not him who eats look down on or despise him who abstains, and let not him who abstains criticize and pass judgment on him who eats; for God has accepted and welcomed him.
>
> Who are you to pass judgment on and censure another's household servant? It is before his own master that he stands or falls. And he shall stand and be upheld, for the Master (the Lord) is mighty to support him and make him stand. One man esteems one day as better than another, while another man esteems all days alike [sacred]. Let everyone be fully convinced (satisfied) in his own mind.
>
> —Romans 14:2-5

Change of any kind seems to be an opportunity for the spirit of strife. A woman in her monthly cycle experiences unusual things because her body and hormones are changing. Many women are difficult to live with during this time. Why? Because things are changing, and she feels different. A lot of family trouble could be avoided if women would get more rest during those times and avoid stressful situations for a few days. Within a few days she might be able to handle wonderfully something that she could not handle at all during the time of her physical changes.

The same situation occurs when middle-aged women go through the change of life. Their bodies are undergoing drastic changes and will no longer do things that they had done all of their lives. These changes affect some women more than others, but for many, it's a season of change that can open doors for strife in relationships. Things a woman was quite satisfied with before may suddenly become unacceptable. Or things that irritated her but were acceptable, she may no longer be willing to endure.

Her patience level is low, and if the noise level is high in the home, strife may be the result. If the husband does not give her the affection she desires she will be more easily hurt. She may withdraw and act in ways that her family is not used to. Her need for affection apart from sex may increase during this time. She wants to be held, but nothing more.

She should remember that her husband cannot read her mind. She is changing, but her family is just the same as always. They do not feel the way she does and should not be expected to understand her without some education.

In going through the change of life myself, I have discovered that just saying to myself, "Joyce, you are feeling these changes, but everything is going to be all right," helps me a lot. Talk to yourself sometimes; have a heart-to-heart conversation with yourself. Do not allow change to disorient you to the point that it causes strife.

When people move, change jobs, lose relationships or make new relationships—and thousands of other types of changes—they are under a certain amount of pressure. Change requires more of our attention than the normal aspects of life. To accommodate the need for more attention to the change, other things may have to suffer loss or be readjusted.

Whenever you are facing changes of any kind, remember the devil will try to take advantage of you. He hopes to catch you off guard so you will let him in without realizing what's happening. Watch for the spirit of strife and refuse to give place to it.

People want change, yet they are afraid of it in many instances. Change means dealing with the unknown. We like to have all our ducks in a row and know exactly what's happening each step of the way. For instance, when you are developing new relationships with people, you must learn how they react in every situation. What things do they like, and what do they dislike? What is acceptable to say to them, and what is not? Will they get offended if you tease them?

Developing a new relationship requires more energy than

being with someone you have known for a long time. It can be stressful, often shortening your fuse in other areas. Beware of strife during times of change.

Another change that can open the door for strife occurs at those times when God is changing you. God changes us in ever-increasing degrees of glory. (See 2 Corinthians 3:18.) Hebrews 12 teaches us that God chastens us for our ultimate good, but while the chastening is taking place, it isn't much fun.

> For the time being no discipline brings joy, but seems grievous and painful; but afterwards it yields a peaceable fruit of righteousness to those who have been trained by it [a harvest of fruit which consists in righteousness—in conformity to God's will in purpose, thought, and action, resulting in right living and right standing with God].
>
> —HEBREWS 12:11

The chastisement changes us and makes us more like Jesus in our thoughts, words and actions. The next verses tell us how we should react when God chastens us.

> So then, brace up and reinvigorate and set right your slackened and weakened and drooping hands and strengthen your feeble and palsied and tottering knees, and cut through and make firm and plain and smooth, straight paths for your feet [yes, make them safe and upright and happy paths that go in the right direction], so that the lame and halting [limbs] may not be put out of joint, but rather may be cured.
>
> —HEBREWS 12:12–13

A footnote to the thirteenth verse in the Worrell New Testament reads as follows:

> Make straight paths for your feet; choose God's word to be a "lamp to your feet, and a light to your path" (Ps.

> 119:105, WNT); not only for your good and the glory of God, but also on account of others, who will be helped or injured by your example.

These instructions show us how to respond to times of chastisement and change (times when God is changing us). The instructions continue in verse 14, where we are to "strive to live in peace with everybody and pursue that consecration and holiness without which no one will [ever] see the Lord." While you are pursuing holiness and allowing God to work in you and change you, remember to strive to live in peace with everybody.

Sometimes we feel confused when God is dealing with us because we do not understand all the things we are feeling inside. Dave and I have learned to tell each other when we believe that God is dealing with us. We might say, "God is dealing with me. I don't know about what yet, but I know something is going on inside me, so if I act a little unusual or seem quieter, that's why."

Before we started doing that, times of personal change often turned into open doors for strife. If Dave did not understand why I was acting strange, and I did not bother to tell him the reason, he would become quiet. Then I thought something was wrong with him. That aggravated me even more, because I thought I already had enough to deal with without him getting weird on me.

Surely you can see how the devil will take advantage of times like this if there is no communication or self-control. Another thing I finally learned was that I did not have the right to display every feeling I had. If God is changing me, I must let Him do it without becoming melodramatic and making a lot more out of the situation than it warrants.

Suffering in silence is good for us. We can learn to go through the changes God brings into our lives without taking our frustrations out on others. We can, and should, learn to bear the good fruit of the Holy Spirit during times of change. Communicate what is needful, but go on about your business and let God do what He needs to do. The more you fight, the longer it's going to take. Sometimes we pray for God to change us, and then wrestle with Him when He tries. We want change, but we're frightened by it.

Change Brings Progress

Changes are designed to bring progress, and Satan will always fight progress. He will oppose you persistently if you are going forward. When God is dealing with you inside, it is intended to bring change outside. God's plan is to bring you into a new realm of glory, but Satan delights in getting you distracted and preventing you from pressing in with God.

There have been numerous times when the Lord dealt with me about some particular, wrong behavior—something I deeply wanted deliverance from and was sincere about pressing through to a place of freedom. Often as I studied and prayed, I could sense I was about to break through, but then havoc would break out in my life instead.

The havoc would make me forget all about what God was working out in me, and I would start attending to my problems. Several weeks or months later, the Holy Spirit would begin dealing with me on that same issue again. Then I would remember that I had been so close to freedom before, and had unknowingly allowed Satan to distract me and get me off track. Often, the "problem" that the devil used was something that opened a door for strife, either within me or someone else.

I sincerely believe this is an area that deserves much attention. Meditate on this, and I believe you may see a similar thread running through your life. Have you noticed that when you try to go forward in some area, Satan uses strife in another area to retard your progress?

I believe we are approaching a time in the body of Christ when we will see a great deal of physical healings. I have had confirmation about this from other people in ministry who also sense God leading in that direction.

During my years in ministry, I have found that the Holy Spirit shows me things on the horizon ahead of time so I can begin preparing myself in that area. Preparation is vital to being used by God. Since I could, in this instance, see what is ahead, I knew I needed to start studying, praying and seeking God in the area of healing the sick.

I heard from God about how He wanted me to proceed, and I began. Within twenty-four hours, I opened up four opportunities for strife. At first, I didn't realize what was happening, which is exactly what Satan wants. Deception means the enemy has control, and we do not know what is happening. In one day, three employees needed some serious correction. I do not mean to imply that any of these people involved are "bad" people. It is just the way Satan operates; he stirs up anything he can to get us distracted. He uses strife to prevent our progress. He will try to work through whatever weaknesses a person has (and we all have some) at a time when we are about to break through into a brand-new glory in our lives.

All three employees are precious people who have hurts and wounds in their past that they are working through. We are trying to help them, and in doing so we must deal with issues from time to time. They have been wounded emotionally, and sometimes their emotions get a bit out of hand. The enemy knows he can push the right buttons and stir up their emotions.

Eventually this weakness will be controlled by the Holy Spirit and become a strength for these people. But for now, it's still an area that Satan can use if they are not aware of his cunning manipulation. Since they work for us, if he gets them stirred up, I end up having to deal with it. It was obvious to me that "unseen" forces were at work when all three individuals happened to have a problem on the same day.

Within the same twenty-four hours I also had a golden opportunity for strife with my husband. It involved our son and our differing opinions on how to handle a situation with him. All parents have to deal with these situations from time to time. I felt one way, and Dave felt another. It was not a long-term problem, but each time it came up, I had to sit on my emotions and remember that Dave is the head of our household.

When we disagree, I can say what I think in a respectful manner, but then, I need to leave the final decision to him and remain at peace. Even though I know what I should do, doing it still requires a certain amount of my attention. Therefore, Satan arranged for this particular instance to occur precisely at a time when he knew it could upset me and initiate strife with my husband.

The devil certainly does not want me to progress in a healing ministry. He does not want me to study and gain new revelation. He does not want me to help more people and see their suffering relieved. He fights against the church and her progress with many things, but strife is one of his favorite deceptive weapons. We make the mistake of thinking that *people* are the problem, when our true enemy is the *spirit of strife.*

It's wise to be watchful, not allowing Satan to use our problems to hinder the work of the Lord in another person's life. No wonder Matthew 26:41 says that we are to "watch and pray." We must watch ourselves and watch how the enemy is trying to work through other people and circumstances to prevent our progress.

What was I to do in these four situations? It was my responsibility to deal with the issues at hand, but it was also important that I keep pressing forward in my study concerning healing the sick. I needed to deal with each individual involved in a godly way, not allowing myself to get all upset and aggravated about it.

Sometimes I do get aggravated with something that needs to be dealt with. Dave has often told me that if I would spend the time dealing with the issue that I spend being upset about it, it would be taken care of and finished. He is right, of course, but it has been a learning process for me.

I finally had to learn that anyone who has to deal with a lot of other people will always have things to handle. That does not mean the people are bad; it's just the way life is. God wants us to walk in love and support one another, edifying and strengthening each other and promoting one another's progress.

Satan wants strife, arguing, judgment, offense and weakness. He knows that he can weaken the strength of any group by bringing division. I need to pray and trust God to lead me to say the right things to them. I don't need to spend all day and night mentally "rehearsing" what I will say to them. Satan wants to fill my mind with just such useless thoughts.

How often do we spend hours rehearsing our words to someone we need to confront, and when the time comes we do not say any of it? All that "mental time" was wasted. We could have spent the same time meditating on the Word or thinking about the goodness of God.

If we trust the Lord, He will lead us in what we are to say at the right time. I should give a reasonable amount of thought to what I say in order to be properly prepared, but getting out of balance allows the devil to waste my time and prevent my progress.

Remember that the devil may try to use strife to prevent you from going forward during times of change. Times of change are often hard, but they lead us into new realms of glory. Watch and pray, and be wise to the enemy's strategies and deceits.

CHAPTER 20
THE STRESS OF CHANGE

Changes at home, at work and at church can produce enormous stress. If you're struggling with such changes, you can experience victory without getting into strife.

1. Have you experienced change in the recent past or present that has been difficult to deal with? Explain why. __________

____

____

2. Is your opposition to certain changes based upon your own opinions or upon God's Word? __________________

____

____

3. Did you or have you given the changes enough time to see if they will work for you? __________________

____

____

4. Explain how you attempted to approach the changes with an open mind. __________________

____

____

____

5. How were the changes good for the organization or social situation as a whole? __________________

____

____

6. Are you willing to speak with those in leadership about your feelings instead of sharing them with everyone else?

____

7. If you are no longer able to be happy in the situation because of the changes that have taken place, do you love

the organization and its people enough to be willing to leave rather than cause strife?

8. Describe a time when God was making changes in you that was particularly stressful.

9. Describe how you "suffered in silence" or took out your frustrations upon others around you.

10. If your behavior created strife, suppose you could go back and change history. How would you rewrite the script?

11. When have you been attacked by a spirit of strife and saw the problem only as being caused by an individual? Explain.

12. How will you go through change and other stressful situations in the future with less strife?

Lord, I surrender my life to You in all my seasons and situations of changes—both past, present and future. Keep me from allowing change to bring me into strife. Help me to draw nearer to You during times and seasons of change. Let me sense Your strength, Your power and Your peace during such times. And Lord, when I need extra help to stay calm and peaceful, please help me to draw a little closer to Your heart. In Jesus' name, amen.

Epilogue

United We Stand, Divided We Fall

During the writing of this book, I noticed an increased attack from the spirit of strife. I had more opportunities to be in strife than usual. I found myself wondering, *What is going on?* It actually took me until I was almost finished writing the book to realize that Satan was attacking me with strife. He was obviously hoping to either distract me, or have me write it with strife in my own heart, so there would be no anointing on it.

Little things that usually do not bother me at all, things over which I was given victory long ago, began to annoy me. I had to make a decision to forgive and not be in strife.

During two of our seminars, we had some friction between team members. Two of our employees in the office had strife between them that we needed to help them settle.

Other situations occurred, all minor, but had they not been properly dealt with, they could have turned into major problems. As I close this book, I want to remind you of the first principle for overcoming strife: Learn to recognize and deal with strife.

If you do not recognize it, it will rip your life apart and you will blame your trouble on everything other than the true root of your problems. When you do recognize it, you must deal with it. If left unconfronted, it will destroy you.

No person is immune to attack. In Luke chapter 4, Jesus Himself was tempted and tried by the devil in the wilderness.

> And when the devil had ended every [the complete cycle of] temptation, he [temporarily] left Him [that is, stood off from Him] until another more opportune and favorable time.
>
> —Luke 4:13

The principles about strife and its dangers have been established in my heart and life for quite a number of years, but Satan certainly saw the writing of this book as an opportune time to try me once again. I am sharing these things with you because I want you to understand that Satan frequently uses strife in an attempt to bring destruction into our lives.

Standing against the spirit of strife has strengthened my understanding and recognition of it. I believe that now I will be stronger than ever against the enemy. When you exercise your faith in any area, it makes it stronger.

During a seminar on the spirit of offense, I asked a group of people to keep a record of how often they had opportunity to get into strife or become offended. One woman reported that she had forty opportunities in one week. This sounds amazing but might actually be a low number compared to some people.

A devastating round of strife can start from a very minor incident. Proverbs 17:14 says, "The beginning of strife is as when water first trickles [from a crack in a dam]; therefore stop contention before it becomes worse and quarreling breaks out."

If you think you have offended someone, go the extra mile and simply say, "If I have offended you, I apologize." Then, if you discover that they indeed were offended, simply ask them to forgive you. The power of the words, "Please forgive me," is amazing! Should the individual refuse to forgive you, at least you have done your part and can dwell in peace.

If someone has offended you, forgive them—and do it quickly. Protect your heart. Proverbs 4:23 reminds us:

> Keep and guard your heart with all vigilance and above all that you guard, for out of it flow the springs of life.

A powerful flow of life will emanate from a heart full of God's Word, but the heart must be protected from bitterness and strife. Resist the devil at his onset. Do not wait to see how serious the problem will become. Treat strife like the plague! Realize that Satan is lurking around, looking for any crack to crawl through. His goal is division!

> Any kingdom that is divided against itself is being brought to desolation and laid waste, and no city or house divided against itself will last or continue to stand.
>
> —MATTHEW 12:25

This scripture depicts the destruction that is taking place while the strife is in progress. In essence, it says that the house, family, church, business, kingdom or city that is divided is brought to desolation and waste. Such a place will not continue to stand. It may last for a period of time, but it will not abide forever.

I believe our family will abide forever through the legacy of the Word of God when the Lord calls us home. I believe our ministry will endure and that our children and grandchildren will carry it from generation to generation because it has been built and maintained on a foundation of peace. I am also acutely aware of the continual opportunities for strife and division, and how we must remain determined to keep strife out.

You have a unique call upon your life. You are an important part of the body of Christ. God has pre-arranged for you to have a powerful and productive life. Jesus paid for it. It is yours unless you allow the devil to steal it from you.

You should leave a legacy to the world and complete the work that He has called you to. The anointing of God is upon you for whatever your task. Don't block the flow by allowing strife in your life. Be all that God has called you to be. Live at peace with yourself, with God and with your fellowman.

> But refuse (shut your mind against, have nothing to do with) trifling (ill-informed, unedifying, stupid) controversies over ignorant questionings, for you know that they foster strife and breed quarrels. And the servant of the Lord must not be quarrelsome (fighting and contending). Instead, he must be kindly to everyone and mild-tempered [preserving the bond of peace].
>
> —2 Timothy 2:23–24

Notes

Chapter One
Exposing Strife

1. *New Riverside University Dictionary* (Boston, MA: The Riverside Publishing Company, 1994), s.v. "strife."

Chapter Two
What Doors Open for Strife?

1. W. E. Vine, Merrill F. Unger and William White, Jr., *An Expository Dictionary of Biblical Words* (Nashville, TN: Thomas Nelson Publishers, 1984), s.v. "*eris*," 2054.

Chapter Nine
How Strife Affects Your Health

1. Archibald D. Hart, *The Hidden Link Between Adrenaline and Stress* (Dallas, TX: Word Books, 1986), 21-23.

Bibliography

Strong, James. *The New Strong's Exhaustive Concordance of the Bible.* Nashville, TN: Thomas Nelson Publishers, 1990.

Vine, W. E., *Vine*'s *Complete Expository Dictionary of Old And New Testament Words.* Nashville, TN: Thomas Nelson Publishers, 1985.

Webster's *II New Riverside University Dictionary.* Boston, MA: Houghton Mifflin Company, 1994.

Hart, Archibald D. *The Hidden Link Between Adrenaline and Stress.* Dallas, TX: Word Books, 1986.

About the Author

Joyce Meyer has been teaching the Word of God since 1976 and in full-time ministry since 1980. As an associate pastor at Life Christian Center in St. Louis, Missouri, she developed, coordinated and taught a weekly meeting known as "Life In The Word." After more than five years, the Lord directed her to establish her own ministry—Life In The Word, Inc.

Her *Life In The Word* radio broadcast is heard on more that 250 stations worldwide. Her thirty-minute television program, *Life In The Word with Joyce Meyer,* was released in 1993 and is broadcast throughout the United States and Canada. Her teaching tapes are enjoyed internationally, and she travels extensively, conducting conferences and speaking in local churches.

Joyce and her husband, Dave Meyer, business administrator at Life In The Word, have been married for more than thirty years and are the parents of four children.

Joyce believes God has called her to establish believers in His Word. After finding freedom and victory in her own life by applying God's Word, Joyce goes equipped to set captives free and to exchange ashes for beauty.

Joyce has taught on emotional healing and related subjects all over the country. She has over 150 different cassette albums on various topics available to help the body of Christ.

Cassette Tape Series Available

Emotional Healing Package:
Confidence; Beauty for Ashes (includes a syllabus); *Managing Your Emotions; Bitterness, Resentment and Unforgiveness* and *Root of Rejection*

Family Revival Kit:
(24 hours of teaching on relationships)
Marriage Volume I; Understanding Your Mate's Personality (includes two personality tests); *Shaping the Lives of Your Children; Marriage Volume II* (includes a syllabus); *Exposing Strife* and *Love One Another*

Mental Strongholds and Mind-sets
Wilderness Mentality
The Wandering, Wondering Mind
The Power of Thought
The Mind of the Flesh

Books Available Written by Joyce Meyer

Tell Them I Love Them
Peace
The Most Important Decision You Will Ever Make
Why, God, Why?
When, God, When?
Beauty for Ashes
The Root of Rejection
Battlefield of the Mind
The Word, the Name, the Blood
If Not for the Grace of God
Enjoying Where You Are on the Way to Where You Are Going
Expect a Move of God . . . Suddenly
Do It! Afraid
Me and My Big Mouth!

For information or to order books or tapes from Joyce Meyer, write to:

Joyce Meyer
Life In The Word, Inc.
P. O. Box 655 • Fenton, MO 63026
Phone: 636-349-0303